I0157837

GET UP

THE FIGHT IS NOT OVER!

Punches thrown in every fight have purpose. Each blow is intended to test us, forcing us to prove what we are made of, challenging us to make our next decision. When life knocks us down, we can choose to lay there, surrender and quit, or realize our need for Christ, his availability and his willingness to be in our corner…

Stacey W. Neal, MDiv

PURPLE CHAIR BOOKS
AND EDUCATIONAL PRODUCTS, LLC.
TRANSFORMATION AND RENEWAL STARTS IN THE MIND, ONE THOUGHT AT A TIME

PCB

Published by Purple Chair Books and Educational Products, LLC

First Printing, 2022

Copyright © Stacey W. Neal, 2022

Neal, Stacey 1972-

Get Up: The Fight Is Not Over!

By Stacey W. Neal

ISBN: 978-1-953671-03-5

Christian Life/ Spiritual 1.Title Printed in the United States of America

Set in xxxxx xxxxx xxxxxx

Designed by xxx xxx

Contents

Forward

Let me be honest, life is hard. Without exception, at some point, we all face experiences that demand our greatest strengths, energies, grit, and fight. Throughout our lives, we will face good days, bad days, and everything in between. No matter who you are, where you have been, or where you come from, you will be required to fight for your place and every success you attain along the way. The experience of life is repeated series of continuous scrimmages and fights, challenges, and opportunities to get it right. Without question, success demands that you show up each time. There are no exceptions. We all must get up again and again. We cannot stay down. We cannot surrender. Even when we get hurt, we cannot throw in the towel. The prophet said in Job 1:1-2, "Mortals, born of woman, are of few days and full of trouble. They spring up like flowers and wither away; like fleeting shadows, they do not endure." Challenges and struggles are a part of life. Not one of us can escape them. However, we never have to endure them or experience them alone. God is with us, and available to all. Any and everyone can call on Him. He does not show partiality. Lovingly, he grants each of us the right and opportunity to experience and receive his very best. Nothing can hinder the power and purpose of God. He will never reject anyone that calls on him. That is the promise of his never-failing and eternal word.

The Bible tells us that all good and perfect gifts come from the Lord. It is his will and good pleasure to do amazing things in our lives. He desires nothing more than to stand with us in every battle, conflict, and fight. God loves us far more than we can fully understand. His love is beyond comprehension. The question is asked in Psalm 8:4-6, "what are mere mortals that you should think about them, human beings that you should care for them? Yet you made them only a little lower than angels and crowned them with glory and honor. You gave them charge of everything you made, putting all things under their authority." God wants us to have everything. He wants to be the source of our inspiration. He wants to be the voice that leads us. He wants to be regarded and known to be the trusted friend you can depend on, the every ready and available coach. That reality has been so well conveyed and presented in the pages of this amazing and insightful little book.

With over thirty years of pastoral ministry, it excites me to discover that there are still talented, dedicated, and faithful young men committed to introducing the lost and hurting to the truth of God's word. This book does just that. With practical, insightful, and magnificent transparency, the author makes plain the fact that God not only cares but that he desperately wants us to win. He does not only want us to win, but he wants each of us to be victorious in Christ Jesus. He wants us to be Champions for Christ. The author portrays God in an exceptional and personal way. He moves God from out there and brings him close. In every situation, he places the God of the universe in our corner.

Using the analogy of a boxer in the ring, the author paints a vivid picture. He allows the reader to see and imagine themselves engaged in a continuous and fierce physical and spiritual battle, a fight. Convincingly, the author succeeds in drawing the reader closer and closer to the point of decision. Strategically and masterfully, he hammers home ideas and points out that a life-transforming decision must be made regarding Christ. He makes it convincingly clear that wisely, we all must choose Christ as either Savior and Lord, companion and friend, or at least the trusted voice in the ring corner. No reader walks away unchallenged or unchanged. No seeker can peruse these pages and not be impacted in some meaningful way. What a blessing this book will be to so many.

I am enthusiastically proud of the work and authenticity that has gone into this piece. I know the countless hours, lonely nights, and sacrifice necessary to produce such a project quite well, having written several books myself. I am grateful for the genuine and heartfelt experiences shared. I am captured by the rawness and candor in which every story is told. Reading through this manuscript, I could not help but reflect on my past, vivid memories, and the moment God transformed me and revealed the brightness of his marvelous light. I share a kindred spirit with the author. He is my brother. I know well from wince he came and all that God has done and is doing. This book is a testament to God's grace, power, and inconceivable plans. I am immeasurably proud and inspired by the level of discipline, tenacity, and courage that went into creating this literary dream. As a fellow reader, student, and traveler, I encourage you to sit back, thoroughly consider what is being presented, and not only apply these shared principles and ideas to your own life but share this transformative message with someone else. I pray that you make the wise and obvious choice and decision for Christ. I am confident your choices will yield immeasurable and inconceivable dividends, resulting in tremendous transformation not only in your life but also in the lives of those around you.

Dr. David Scott
Pastor/Educator
USA, Army Chaplain (retired)

Dedication

I would like to dedicate this book to my mother, Mary Ann Neal-Bernard. Thank you for having the courage to dream big and drive forward in faith. You took the leap of faith to travel from Belize, Central America, to start a new life in a foreign land. Your life struggle has taught me how to work hard and thank God for everything. Your life taught me that Jesus Christ will keep and care for me through all the seasons of life. There were many times I have seen you cry, but I have never seen you quit.

After so many years of toil and labor, you still joyfully help others. You have always lived your belief that "it's in giving that we receive". Growing up in poverty, the generosity of others has fuels your tireless concern for others. God has made you a "Champion for Christ". I want to honor you with this book, like a rose presented to the Queen of the Beauty Pageant. I present to you this rose while you still live. Let it be to you a token of my love and appreciation for every sacrifice you made to give me the best life you could, and for raising me. Please accept this rose, and I pray as your son that my life has and continues to make you smile. Although the journey has been long, with many twists, bumps, and turns, your prayers lead me to Christ, and he put my life on the right track. Thank you for your tirelessly prayers for my protection while I was lost and wondering aimlessly in the wilderness. If life was a string of single photographs, you deserve to be called "Momma Paparazzi", because you have shown me the importance of "capturing" every precious moment.

Acknowledgment

I stand on the shoulders of many great people who took the time to help me throughout my life. Thank you for helping in my development through your words, thoughts, and deeds. I believe divine intervention has sustained and preserved me for such a time as this. To each and every one of you, thank you. It is my prayer that God pour a double portion of blessings into your lives. Additionally, I would like to address my best friend and a very special person in my life. Thank you to the moon and back again!

With the greatest level of sincerity and enthusiasm, I would like to acknowledge and applaud my partner, supporter, companion, and adoring wife, First Lady Dana Monique Neal. You are the queen of our castle and the true blessing I have found. Thank you for supporting my journey to Pastor, Army Chaplaincy, and our growing ministry. God has proven that He always knows best. I am so grateful and overwhelmingly blessed now and the moment you came into my life. I am humbled and thankful for God's plan to join us in the union of husband and wife. You are worthy and deserve to be cherished and cared for through God's love and power. I do not have enough or adequate words to thank you for your effort, intentionality, and hard work to keep our family strong. Many see the front, but never behind the scenes or all you do in the rear.

The years of challenges and struggles have strengthened and cemented our bond of love. Through days and nights of heartache and shared tears, Christ Jesus has kept us together. You are an amazing woman of God, wife, and outstanding mother to our children. Thank you for joining me on this journey, coming alongside me, stepping into the ring with God, and being a Godly wife in my corner. I love you today, tomorrow, and forevermore.

Introduction

I came to The Lord broken. *I was* spiritually poor, financially penniless, pitifully prideful, emotionally in pain, and smashed in pieces, *but God* bestowed His grace, mercy, and immeasurable gifts upon me. With each breath, I experience the wondrous realization of God's peace, perspective, and promise. With God's gift of exhortation, let me encourage you by saying, "It's a brand-new blessing; it's another day journey and a fresh beginning on this side of heaven."

I have learned from my own experiences that life can be *rough*. However, when you realize you are rolling with God, the one in control of everything, you discover the capacity and courage to face another day. Glory to God for all able to testify to the goodness and liberty of the Lord through whom we now experience new life. "Unspeakable Joy" flows from the hearts of believers who can give firsthand testimony of Christ's power and ability to declare freedom from every type and form of spiritual bondage. Praises be unto God for those seeking divine wisdom, spiritual insight, and supernatural ability to unlock the power of the Holy Spirit in their lives. To God be all glory and honor, Amen.

CHAPTER ONE

It Has Been a Fight just to Get There

Y ou must never forget that you are a winner! Winning is in your DNA. What do you mean, Pastor Neal? Well, let me explain. You see, from inception, you were in a fight to be born. From the beginning, you were in a fight to the death against your father's other seeds, all competing to take your place, joining with your mother's egg. This fight was a defining moment, life or death. This scenario was a matter of one shot, hit or miss, within a small window of opportunity. This was truly a contest of wins or losses. The fact that you are reading this book speaks inarguably to the fact that you won the competition. It is a testimony that you survived your "Scenario of Struggle" (S.O.S) to become a *Living Champion.*

Let us examine some of the dynamic highlights of God's stellar performance to get you here on earth. God placed you as close to the egg as possible, yet a gap existed between the goal and achievement. It was the working in the midst of the unseen that created your life that is now seen by all. Simply put, God has a methodology and way of working on the situations and issues of our lives in secret, long before anyone else gets a glimpse of you. *God's grace consistently and purposely leads you from the place of Go to the Goal, and over every Gap or delay by the wisdom and power of His divine Guidance.*

God operates methodically and intentionally. I like to call this the *5G Principle*. If *God,* the great and matchless sovereign of the universe has ordained you to *go* to accomplish his desired *goals,* then you can be assured He will direct and lead you over obstacles, challenges, and *gaps* by His divine *guidance*. He will not abandon you or leave you alone. If God has called you to it, by the power of His Spirit, He will help you to accomplish it. Remember, God does not make mistakes. He knows all things. There is nothing outside His knowing. God cannot be surprised. Please do not miss this. This is life-changing counsel, understanding, and spiritual wisdom to grasp, leading to success through the Holy Spirit. In no way do I wish to waste your time. However, I do wish to help you grow and win bigger through God's spirit and divine leading. What good is it for you to read this book and not get anything from it? Now that I have presented to you spiritual principles given to me by God through His spirit for both our benefits, it deserves a visual or diagram to help you better understand and digest what has been suggested. Let us take a look at our diagram.

God's Guidance

Go-------------------------------------Goals

Gaps

This diagram is a physical and visual reminder that whatever God has called you to do, He is big, capable, powerful, and wise enough to achieve through you. I suggest that you do whatever necessary to ingrain this inarguable truth deep into your mind, heart, subconscious, and soul. So you do not forget, I recommend that you place this diagram wherever it can be readily available, tangible, and visibly accessible. I suggest you crop it, Snap Chat it, Instagram it, Facebook (Metaverse) it, YouTube it, save it, frame it, put it on the refrigerator, mirror, vision board, work desk, car dashboard, kitchen countertop, PC gaming unit, make it a bookmarker, save it as a screen saver, text it to a friend, and say it to yourself over and over again. Repeat after me: "Every day of life is a blessing, the granting of new and never before seen or experienced opportunities. God is gracious and lovingly kind toward me. Today I have been granted the Green light of favor to "*Go*", and live for the glory of God. Because the Eternal father, who is *God,* is above me, and my *Gaps* are beneath me, I will let go and let God *guide* me in the right way and the paths I should take to accomplish His intended *Goals*, AMEN.

Chapter Two

You Were Created from the Dust

I t is only by the "Divine Design of God" that you could live and thrive beyond the days of dependency on the nutrients from your mother's umbilical cord and milk. Your existence is a testament to the fact you have beaten the inconceivable odds of (1 in 40 million) upwards to (1 in 1.2 billion) of potential seeds. Therefore, it is fair to conclude God made you "intentionally." Divinely, He made each of us capable of immeasurable and unlimited success. No matter the odds or obstacles, because God is with us, we win!

You must understand and embrace the concepts and ideas of winning and being a winner! Let us recap this thought so you more clearly understand and better grasp what is being said. Initially, you required the natural and nutritious nourishment your mother provided for nine months to survive in the womb. Now you need God's spiritual connection and nourishment to thrive and excel in this fallen, depraved, and sinful world. From inception, it was the breath of God that sustained both you and your mother. Following God and remaining close to Him provides the perfect source of life and sustainment. We can do nothing on our own. In Him, we move, live, and have the fullness of our being. It is God's spirit that keeps you alive. The is no argument against the fact, if God can bring you safely from your mother's womb, He can bring you safely through the challenges, obstacles, worries, trappings, and wilds of this dark and wicked world.

The writer says in Genesis 1:26, "Then God said, "Let us make man in Our image, according to Our likeness; and let them *rule over* the fish of the sea and the birds of the sky and the cattle and over ***all the earth***, and over every creeping thing that creeps on the earth. From the very beginning, God created and designed you to be a ruler. Mankind is the only creature in all creation made in the image and likeness of the great and eternal God. In the same way, God, the father, rules the heavens and the universe. From creation, you were meant and intended to rule on the earth. From the dust, you were designed for the dominion of your district as the reigning champion for Christ. God has equipped you to rumble in the fight on the outside but also to rule with the moral likeness of God from within. Because God breathed into the nostrils of man (the human creation), he alone caused us to become living beings and living spirits.

The love of God toward you is matchless. There is nothing good that God will ever withhold from you. He wants you to have, become, and experience the very best as a loving and compassionate father. Although you may have heard this before, you must believe it and allow it to be deposited in your spirit. No matter the situation or circumstance. No matter the challenge, struggle, or seemingly overwhelming defeat, every delay, obstacle, or setback, is nothing more than a divinely orchestrated opportunity for a spectacular and life-transforming testimony and comeback. When God is in control, if life knocks you down, remember the fight is not over until you stand victoriously as Christ's "Champion"!

As the Lord's ambassador and Christ's champion, you must remember and consistently say to yourself, "From the dust I have been created, designed for dominion over all of the earth and every creeping thing"! No matter the scenario, condition, or situation I face, I will rule over it through the power of Christ the living God. This is the will of God concerning my life. Therefore, I am already the victor over every single thing that desires to dominate, control, and have power over me. I am more than a conqueror through Him that loves me. Because of that truth, I will use the 5G Principles to help me over every obstacle and gap I might face as I move toward the divine glory of God". On this journey, you will have opposition from the natural and spiritual realm. This reality demands that you develop a dual mindset to recognize the challenges, battles and fights in both realms. In both the physical (natural) and spiritual realms, there are constant and ever raging battles that must be faced. Daily, in the natural realm, we struggle, fighting the good fight outwardly. Spiritually, we fight inwardly wrestling against temptations, passions, and desires to please and satisfy ourselves, instead of surrendering our will and doing things God's way.

As a follower and ambassador of Christ, you cannot afford to lose or forfeit your connection, identity, and likeness to God. You only need to turn on the TV or scroll your media page, and you will almost immediately see the negative effects of sin and wickedness in the world and countless people who have lost their connection, identity, and moral likeness to the holy and righteous God. Men and women have become their own gods. Now is the time that you must draw a line in the sand, and reclaim your identity, conviction, and righteous connection. It is time to stop imitating people tossed, turned, and governed by their own emotions, impulses, and distorted understanding. You are a child of the great King. You are a member of a Holy nation. If you agree, I need you to say to yourself, "When I was born, God demonstrated and showed His favor toward me. The same God can and will continue to do the same all the days of my life". God takes pleasure in doing amazing things for us. However, He also expects the demonstration of growth and maturity as we walk by faith in and over the gaps.

> **LET US PRAY:** Lord, we come to you as humbly as we can. We pray that you remove the scales from our eyes and let us see that you have created us for righteous ruler over of all creation. When champions of Christ are in positions of power and leaning on your guidance, then all your people prosper. We know this world needs your righteousness. If my battle and fighting in the ring bring honor to your name, let me war and fight with all my heart, spirit, mind, and soul for your glory. Show me and reveal all that I am in you, and teach me to be the best I can be for you. Coach me to be "Christ's Champion" in the hardest fights of my life. Through the power of your spirit, I proclaim with blessed assurance that with Christ in my corner, I know with certainty that God will guide and lead me over every obstacle and gap so that I reach and accomplish His intended goals by His amazing grace. Amen.

CHAPTER THREE

Willing Defenders of the Wall

What is a Gap? That is a great question. I am so glad you asked. The dictionary identifies and defines a gap as missing pieces of the puzzle, a break or hole in an object or between two objects. I asked the LORD, "What does the Bible have to say about gaps?" The spirit moved and lead me to pick up my iPhone and ask my technological companion Siri. Immediately, an article at www.gotquestions.org gave me the answer to my question. Found in Ezekiel 22:30, the Lord says, "I looked for someone among them who would build up the wall and stand before me in the *gap* on behalf of the land so I would not have to destroy it, but I found no one." The word picture painted in this verse is that of a wall with a hole or a *gap* in it. During that period, a wall provided the best and most secure form of protection. A breach in any area of the wall offered an enemy a significant advantage and opportunity. A gap in the wall meant vulnerability. If an enemy attacked, all available forces would have to swarm and concentrate all defenses at the location of the breach. The gap would need to be repaired as soon as possible. Left unattended and unrepaired, the city would inevitably fall.

So often, we feel broken, defeated, and convinced we are losing life's battles. It is during those times we feel, whether we admit it or not, that there is a breach in the wall. We are fighting, but to what avail? The enemy has advanced and broken through the gates. It is during these times and moments of great struggle that we need God the most. It is during these times we need His guidance, leadership, and power. During these times, I suggest you ask God to strengthen, encourage, and awaken the warrior and champion within you. Run to Jesus, let Him coach you through what might be the fight of your life. The enemy has broken through; this is not business as usual. This is not shadow boxing. This is the real fight. Ask God to help you be the one He searched for in Ezekiel 22:30. Stand and fight, rebuild the torn-down wall. You were not created to be defeated. From the beginning, you were destined to rule, reign, and conquer. Defeat only enters and is possible when we abandon or forfeit our identity and connection to Christ.

Sin is the only thing that weakens you and minimizes your ability to defend yourself from your enemies. Have you forgotten that the power of Christ rules and reigns over every Satanic force and power? Jesus Christ has defeated and has authority over sin, death, and the grave. As followers of the Lord Jesus, daily, we are in a fight against a dirty, deceptive, diabolical, but defeated foe. Because Christ has already defeated the serpent, victory belongs to you through the power of the Holy Spirit. It is time to get up! The season of the knockdown is over. God is turning the fight around. He is giving you His favor again. By the power of the Living and Eternal God, I declare "Defeat, your time is over!" We decree that Christ is awakening the champions and warriors within us. We are reclaiming and taking back our position of authority. You have created us to be conquerors, rulers, and victors. We will defend the breach; the city will not fall!" Now, as we conclude this chapter, I would like to go to the Lord in prayer with you.

SHALL WE PRAY? As champions of Christ, we cry out to the Lord in prayer that He would awaken the defender within our hearts and repair our broken walls. Lord Jesus, fortify our lives with unmovable stones. Place us within your strong tower. In your covering, no enemy can infiltrate our dwelling or stand against it. God, prepare and equip us for the hardest fights of our lives. You have designed and prepared the uniforms to be worn in battle, now for your glory, make us victorious. We are confident of your victorious power Lord Jesus, so victory belongs to us. I speak life over every dead situation and freedom to every bound spirit. Now, Lord, I bless and thank you in advance, in Jesus name. Now, if you agree with this prayer, say Amen!

CHAPTER FOUR

Without God, Every Wall Will Crumble

G aps in any area of our lives, particularly our faith, allow the enemy to attack us and gain minimal victories. Our enemies, the devil, and his minions, never rest. They are constantly exploring and searching for unguarded areas and spaces in your life to enter and turn down the remaining walls of hope in your life. By contrast, God wants us to be diligent and committed to repairs, increasing and strengthening our faith. In Him, we are strong. When we run into the safety of His strong tower, we are fortified. Without His covering and protective shelter, we set ourselves up to experience the consequences of gaps and breaches in our walls. Wherever we are vulnerable, that is where the enemy will attack.

Sometimes, God is not visible in the midst of our challenges and struggles. However, He is always there with us, guiding if we listen, showing us how to hold on and mend the broken places in our lives. Lovingly, God creates scenarios and opportunities for us to demonstrate our willingness to trust Him and allow Him to be the coach in our corner. It all begins with a "Yes"! With that simple word, God will help you and empower you with the strength and ability to defend your position. With a "Yes", He will endow you with His matchless and indomitable power through the Holy Spirit. Remember, it was not by military might or strategy but by the power of God that the walls of Jericho fell. This power is still available to you in your desire to have conquest over your enemies. Never forget, the battle is not yours; it belongs to the Lord. You are not cunning enough, fast enough, or strong enough to win life's most difficult battles. You will need the power of God to help in every move you make. It is only through His power that you can defeat your enemies and become a champion for Christ.

The key is listening and obeying. Trough obedience, you become intentional in the development of your spiritual discipline. Spend more time studying God's word and in prayer. Spend time alone meditating and focusing on the word of God. Jesus is the living word that became flesh. Study His word! He speaks to us the loudest and clearest during these periods of silence, meditation, and reflection. Never forget that you are not alone. God is always there. He is the one that never sleeps. His eyes move throughout the whole earth. He knows how to rescue and supply whatever we need. Amid the most challenging circumstance, He has a ram in the bush. He will rescue and always save before it is too late. He is never late but always right on time. Never forget, our God is a miracle worker. Nothing is impossible to Him. All we need is hope, faith, and always to believe. Like I said before, every setback is the opportunity for a tremendous and spectacular comeback.

There is no denial we serve a God who specializes in the impossible. He steps into our situations just in the nick of time. The Lord, our God, is powerful and mighty to save. Through His divine and well-orchestrated plans, He repeatedly proves that only a great God like himself (YHWH) can show out as He does. The writer in Exodus 15:11-12 says "Who is like you among the gods, O LORD— glorious in holiness, awesome in splendor, performing great wonders?

You raised your right hand, and the earth swallowed our enemies." No matter the challenge, hold the wall with courageous faith, and God will cause your enemies to fall before you like the great walls of Jericho. Make the powerful name of Jesus your strong tower and refuge. Understand well what Christ meant by calling you a "Living Stone." You are powerful, active, and committed to the work and life available in Christ Jesus.

Through the power of the Holy Spirit, you have limitless possibilities and strength flowing through you. Facing the mighty giant Goliath, the shepherd boy David said in 1Samuel 17:45-46, "You come to me with sword, spear, and javelin, but I come to you in the name of the LORD of Heaven's Armies—the God of the armies of Israel, whom you have defied. Today the LORD will conquer you, and I will kill you and cut off your head." You are part of the body of Christ, a stone in the eternal wall of a house that will never be breached! When you understand and embrace this inarguable truth, you can and will boldly and courageously declare, "No weapon formed against me shall prosper." With unshakable boldness and rock solid faith you will declare the words of the writer in Psalm 27:1-3, The LORD is my light and my salvation— so why should I be afraid? The LORD is my fortress, protecting me from danger, so why should I tremble? When evil people come to devour me, when my enemies and foes attack me, they will stumble and fall. Though a mighty army surrounds me, my heart will not be afraid. Even if I am attacked, I will remain confident."

Nothing brings me greater joy than to perceive your spiritual growth. God knows the delight it brings to my heart. You are a champion, and I am excited that it is breaking forth. It has, for so long, been waiting to come out. Now is the time. God is ready to reveal the real you. He has done this before. He specializes in transformation. We can look at our brother Peter. His given name was Simon. Jesus changed his name. Knowing what lay inside him, the scriptures say in 1John 1:42, "Looking intently at Simon, Jesus said, "Your name is Simon, son of John—but you will be called Cephas" (which means "Peter")' which is translated "Rock." This new name cast a vision and new perspective, acknowledging and identifying Peter as stable, unmovable, and secure. Jesus saw in Peter the character traits of a leader and champion.

God has created and equipped you to withstand the blows thrown at you. He has given you all you need to be a champion and conqueror. Because He stands for you and with you, you are unbeatable, unbreakable, and invincible. No matter how difficult or hot the battle rages fight with all your might. You will win. Remember the words of the apostle Paul in Ephesians 6: 10-17, "Be strong in the Lord and his mighty power. Put on the full armor of God so that you can take your stand against the devil's schemes. For our struggle is not against flesh and blood, but against the rulers, against the authorities, against the powers of this dark world, and the spiritual forces of evil in the heavenly realms. Therefore put on the full armor of God so that when the day of evil comes, you may be able to stand your ground, and after you have done everything, to stand. Stand firm then, with the belt of truth buckled around your waist, with the breastplate of righteousness in place, and with your feet fitted with the readiness that comes from the gospel of peace. In addition to all this, take up the shield of faith, with which you can extinguish all the flaming arrows of the evil one. Take the helmet of salvation and the sword of the Spirit, which is the word of God."

It is my greatest prayer that this book serves as the missing piece to the puzzle of your success in life. God is always the final factor in the most difficult equation. He is always the source and conclusion to the best possible answer. It is always the best decision to run to Him and to pursue the way of Christ. What better goal and ambition than to be a Champion for Christ? In attempts to present ourselves as patriotic and loyal citizens, we readily run to problems in defense of our towns, cities, states, and country. We know how to fight. God has placed the fighting spirit within us. In the same way, we are equipped to fight spiritually. No one else is coming. We must fight our own battles. We must be our own spiritual first responders. As Christ's champions, we must accept the challenge to defend the walls in our own lives and the lives of others. We are the Lord's ambassadors, children, and His chosen "Living Stones."

LET US PRAY: Lord, teach us to put up that which cannot be torn down. Lord Jesus, we praise you and ask that you would send us the power of the Holy Spirit, so we can repel the assaults and attacks of the enemy. Lord, we know you created us to be living and unmovable stones in the eternal building of the Kingdom of Heaven. You have chosen and ordained us because of the difference we can make when we are used by you. Great God, teach us our value and worth, and please show us your way. We realize you created us for more than we can imagine. Now that we know the value of you placing us like perfectly fitted stones, wherever there is weakness, I pray the enemy meets you O great one in that place. Lord, you are our protection and defense. Teach us to stand and be still. Fill us with your power, and make us witnesses of your wondrous works through us. I ask all these things in Jesus' name, Amen.

CHAPTER FIVE

Give Me a Heart like David's

I love the story of David, hailed as one of the greatest kings in Israel's history. His life is an enduring example of a chosen champion, created to rule and dominate his region and area for God. Even from his youth, David was the Lord's champion. In 1Samuel 17, we find young David going about his routine and daily chores. David was tasked to perform the duties and functions of a shepherd. By contrast, his older brothers served their obligation as Soldiers in the Israeli army. As the youngest, David's father Jesse instructed him to take food to his brothers on the frontline of the battle. At this stage of life, as the little brother, David was the gofer and errand boy. Sometimes we find ourselves tasked with doing things we do not necessarily want to do. We have all had similar experiences. That is just a part of this thing called life. I encourage you to do everything with joy, enthusiasm, and thanksgiving in your heart. You never know why God has willed it, nor His plan. Whenever and wherever God sends you, He has a purpose.

Through his obedience, David walked into a critical moment in history. His willingness to follow his father's instructions brought him close and in direct contact with the military forces of Israel and the Philistines. Unknowingly, David stepped into destiny. Obedience created a situation and scenario that would impact and transform the nation of Israel for thousands of years, ultimately resulting in a little, unknown, and seemingly insignificant little shepherd boy becoming the celebrated king and great grandfather of our blessed Savior, Jesus. The ancient text affirms this in Matthew 1:27, saying, "After Jesus left the girl's home, two blind men followed along behind him, shouting, "Son of David, have mercy on us!"

The scriptures tell us that both armies agreed to send their champion (warrior) to fight in a contest; winner takes all. The purpose of the contest was to minimize bloodshed on both sides. The Philistines presented their champion, Goliath, a muscular mass of 9-foot 4-inches. However, nobody in the army of Israel had the nerve or courage to step into the ring. Have you felt intimated by a problem, situation, or set of circumstances that seemed too large or massive for you to defeat or be victorious? If I can be honest, I have found myself in that situation countless times. But, my faith, confidence, and hope in God compelled me to fight on, seeing it to the end. Let me encourage you. If you feel you are in a season of tremendous and overwhelming battles, keep fighting, never surrender, never quit. No matter the enemy's mass, force, or size standing before you, keep fighting, moving forward, knowing it is not over until God says so! No battle is yours. It belongs to the Lord!

Have you ever found yourself in a situation or set of circumstances where you were unsure if God sent you to be a champion, or are you there now? Be confident; God does not make mistakes. If he sends you, He not only has a plan, but he has prepared and equipped you for the fight. The battle David stepped into was seemingly unfair. There is no fairness in a fight between a little boy and a giant. However, when God is on your side, the victory in the battle is yours before it begins. When it comes to fighting, there is an old saying, "It's not the size of the dog in the fight; more important is the size of the fight in the dog." The size of your faith is what counts. My question to you is simply, "How big is your fight?" If you did not know or have forgotten, the size of your fight is in direct correlation to the size of your faith. Your biggest victory is a result of your faith! The bigger faith you have in God, the bigger the warrior in you. Little faith means little fight, some faith means some fight, but great faith means great victory!

Uniquely, David was a worshiper and warrior. David was ferocious in battle. But he was also sensitive to the spirit and voice of God. He recognized the need for a war cry and posture of prayer and worship in the times of life's greatest fights and battles. We see this in Psalm 144:1-2 when David says, "Praise the LORD, who is my rock. He trains my hands for war and gives my fingers skills for battle. He is my loving ally and my fortress, my tower of safety, my rescuer.

He is my shield, and I take refuge in him. He makes the nations submit to me." Say this with me, *"When God calls me to fight, every giant will fall by His might. No matter how small or Goliath in size, victory and deliverance is always on my side"*. As the Lord's champions, let this be our mantra and war cry as we continue to walk by faith and not by sight. We have been called to walk by the spirit of God regardless of the situation or circumstances. Imagine how much stronger and encouraged you might be if you believed the word of God rather than accept or embrace the limitations and opinions of others or the negative and debilitating self-talk we are all guilty of practicing. If you will only believe, you too will have the testimony of the young David, future king of Israel, who killed Lions, Bears, and giants, Goliath.

Although David experienced a full and rich life, full of highs and lows, he was no less than a three-time champion. Scripture informs us first that he received God's private anointing from the prophet Samuel preparing him for the task. Scripture says in 1Samuel 16:12-13, "Then the LORD said, "Rise and anoint him; this is the one." So Samuel took the horn of oil and anointed him in the presence of his brothers, and from that day on, the Spirit of the LORD came powerfully upon David. He was anointed the second time when he became the king of Judah. Scripture says in 2 Samuel 2:1-4, "David inquired of the LORD, "Shall I go up into any of the cities of Judah?" And the LORD said to him, "Go up." David said, "To which shall I go up?" And he said, "To Hebron." David went up there, and his two wives also, Ahinoam of Jezreel and Abigail, the widow of Nabal of Carmel. And David brought up his men who were with him, everyone with his household, and they lived in the towns of Hebron. And the men of Judah came, and there they anointed David king over the house of Judah." His third anointing was when the Lord elevated him as king over all of Israel. We are told in 2Samuel 5:1-5, "All of the tribes of Israel came to David at Hebron and said, "We are your bone and flesh. Previously, when Saul was king over us, you were the one leading Israel out and in. Also, the LORD said to you: You will shepherd *my* people Israel, and you will be ruler over Israel." So all of the elders of Israel came to the king at Hebron, and King David made a covenant with them before the LORD at Hebron. They anointed David king over Israel. David was thirty years old when he began to reign, and he reigned forty years. He reigned over Judah from Hebron for seven years and six months, and he reigned over all of Israel and Judah from Jerusalem for thirty-three years." David went from the champion of the shepherd fields to the people's champion, the anointed king over all the tribes of Israel. When faith in God is the foundation of your life, there is no limit to what God can do through you.

LET US PRAY: God, you are able and willing to give us a far better life than we could ever imagine. Teach us to have faith like David. You have created us for such a time as this. It is not by chance that we now live. Along this journey, we have all faced Goliath-sized bears, lions, and giants of various sizes. Lord, help us to remember and always know that you are bigger than any challenge we might ever face. Give us your courage. Help us to stand and never quit in the fight. We pray for strength and increased courage. You have shown us through scripture that Jesus has all authority and complete power. We ask that you fan the flames and ignite our faith as never before. Cause us to stand courageously for your name's sake. Make us the champions in our fields, and cause us to find and experience victory because we dare to trust you and hold to your word, Amen.

CHAPTER SIX

Prepare Me for the Fight

D avid's success began with his hope and trust in God. Repeatedly, David was fueled and bolstered by his faith and the understanding that God was the source of his strength in every fight. Throughout all time and space, this fact remains relevant and true. God is the beginning and the end of all strength. David repeatedly proved that the key to winning fights and battles big and small is centered on being spiritually prepared. No matter where life takes us, God remains sovereign and all-powerful. There is no storm so big that God cannot calm. Every believer in Christ must carry this truth buried in their hearts and anchored deep in their spirit and soul. We must never forget that Christ rules and reigns throughout the universe. When we are called to battle, He has already equipped us with everything we need to win. Through His strength and power living within us, we can scorch the earth, and shake up and transform the world.

Spectators perceived David merely on the errand of food delivery. However, in reality, God had sent him on a rendezvous with destiny. God had positioned David, placing him face to face with the enemy of Israel. Although his enemy and foe was big, massive, and intimidating, David accepted the challenge, went into the ring, and emerged the undisputed champ through the power of his God

(YHWH). David's journey to greatness was not a straight one. It took him from Bethlehem down into the low lands of Socoh in the southern part of Judah. There he would face the Philistine's warrior Goliath and discover himself anew. Right now, you might be facing a Goliath-sized problem or situation. Please know that God is more than able to solve it. If He did it for David, He can and will do it for you if you trust Him and stand boldly in your faith. The story of David teaches us to fight by faith, no matter how impossible the situation looks. We are reminded in scripture that the just will live by their faith, telling us in Hebrew 11:6 "without faith it is impossible to please him (God): for he that comes to God must believe that he is, and that he is a rewarder of them that diligently seek him."

Although justified in being intimidated by the size, ferociousness, and reputation of the giant Goliath, David's confidence remained in the power of his God. Remembering success defending his sheep and slaying the Lion and the Bear, David realized all enemies fall at the hands of those who trust in Yehovah. Following David's example, we, too, must believe that God will use us as His instrument to defeat every Goliath in our lives. Through God's power, all things are possible. Stir up the gift of faith that lay within you. Reflect on past victories, and decisive battles won. You must remember and recount the great and powerful moves of God at important times in your life. You have never won a single battle or fight in your strength. You have never entered a ring without someone in your corner. God has always been there. It has always been his sweet and gentle tugging and whisper leading. He will never leave you alone.

If you are still reading this book, by now, you should be convinced that as the Lord's Soldiers, we are in a continuous battle. Daily the warfare rages. However, more important, you are still in the fight, committed and willing to do your part, holding on, and never giving up. As good Soldiers, we are invested in not merely being in the ranks, but unsheathing our swords and saying "En Garde", the French phrase used to warn opposing fencers to get ready, engage, and begin the battle. As Christians, we should always be spiritually prepared and in a fighting posture in defense against the imminent attacks of our enemies. As skilled warriors, daily, we must stand ready for spiritual warfare, swords in hand, advancing and screaming "En Garde" at the enemy's approach because we are always ready to fight!

Looking at David, we discover he alone had the fighting spirit and the "faith to fight"! Interestingly, being a boy, he was not a Soldier of Israel or a trained warrior. He was a little insignificant Shepherd on an errand to deliver food to his brothers. Realizing fear had crippled Israel's army, God moved on David's faith and his memory of past victories. The right thoughts determine decisions, movement, and actions. Battles are won in the mind and heart before the fighting begins. I challenge you to develop and cultivate the mind of a warrior and champion. Seek the Lord in prayer. Ask him for His power. Petition the Lord for a heart, mind and spirit like David's. Remember all that God has done in your life. Reflect on the fact He has brought you from there to here and taken you from here to there. Remember all the wonderful things He has already done, and continues to do on your behalf. David's faith was built on the testimony of a solid and proven track record. A young David said in 1 Samuel 17:36, "Your servant has killed both the lion and the bear, and this uncircumcised Philistine will be like one of them since he has taunted the armies of the living God."

David provides a stellar example and blueprint. We need his enthusiasm and the kind of faith that strengthens and encourages us when facing our foes in battle and warfare. I pray the Lord prepare and teach us to fight by faith, allowing us to strike and tear down our adversaries with the eternal sting of His holy power. I pray that He teach us to fight in confidence. Like David, let us break and destroy every doubt. In boldness, David said in 1Samuel 17:45, "You come to me with a sword, a spear, and a javelin. But I come to you in the name of the Lord of hosts, the God of the armies of Israel, whom you have taunted."

Although the attacks of the enemy can be crippling, I plead with you to remember this. As a child of God, you are never alone. Your enemies are God's enemies. When you fight, He fights for you. Those who wage war against you are actually waging war against God. They cannot win. God fights for His people; He never leaves them abandoned. However, He searches for His champion, someone He can use. David says this in 1Samuel 17: 47-48 "Today *the LORD will conquer you*, and I will kill you and cut off your head. And then I will give the dead bodies of your men to the birds and wild animals, and the whole world will know that there is a God in Israel! And everyone assembled here will know that **the LORD rescues his people**, but not with sword and spear. **This is the LORD's battle** and he will give you to us!" Wake up from your spiritual slumber. God is with you. He is a great warrior. The Lord God mighty in battle is His name! Speak life and power to your faith. You will live and not die. You are the Lord's champion. Go and win for the glory of God!

> **LET US PRAY:** Lord, help us to see that you have equipped us for every good work. You have given us the tools to face the hardest battles. Give us the battle songs of David, who believed in the name of the Lord of hosts, and that God intended His people to be victors over their enemies. Awaken the champion within us. Teach us to exercise our faith daily. Make us your champions, and train us to fight mightily in the spirit. We get knocked down, but you raise us again. Help us stand our ground. When we fight, let us win more and more territory. Make us your victors. Reveal to us all that we are. Let us dominate every area in your name. When we fall, lift us from the Canvas. Tired, bloodied, and scarred, help us to keep fighting, crying, "Make me a champion" for Christ, Amen.

CHAPTER SEVEN

Christ, the Coach in Your Corner

Since the beginning, God has been in man's corner, talking, guiding, and instructing him and her to ensure them the very best. The first man "Adam," was created to rule and have dominion. Unlike any other creature, Adam was made in the divine image of God. The only equal or parallel to this jewel of creation was taken out of him, called woman, who the man Adam called "Eve" his companion and partner in the fulfillment of God's intended plan of man's dominion on earth. The scriptures record in Genesis 2:18, 21-23 "The LORD God said "It is not good for the man to be alone. I will make a helper suitable for him." So the LORD God caused the man to fall into a deep sleep; and while he was sleeping, he took one of the man's ribs and then closed up the place with flesh. Then the LORD God made a woman from the rib he had taken out of the man, and he brought her to the man. The man said, "This is now bone of my bones and flesh of my flesh; she shall be called 'woman, for she was taken out of man.""

From scripture, we discover God's intimacy and closeness to man (humankind). Since the garden, God has been there. He has never been too far away to hear or too busy to ignore. He has never left us alone. He never has nor will He ever abandon us. We are the crown of His creation and precious in His sight. He loves us and is in love with us. He will never deny us. Those that hope in Him can rely on His faithfulness. No matter the scenario, He will never treat us like strangers because we are His friends. We are more than pitiful beggars, weary travelers, and orphans. We are the sons and daughters of God. The Lord, our God, has made us; we have not made ourselves.

From the beginning, the God of the universe has walked, talked, and communed with those He loves. Daily, Yahweh was with Adam in the garden. Although God created Adam and gave him dominion over the earth, He did not leave him alone. He was in Adam's corner, teaching, instructing, leading, and encouraging him. Routinely, God provided Adam with necessary and needed counsel to achieve and accomplish every task he was given. If we would only listen, we too, have the spirit and word of God to lead us, teach us, instruct us, guide us, and encourage us in every situation and circumstance. Affirming the necessity and power of God's word, the writer says in Psalm 119:105, "Your word is a lamp to guide my feet and a light for my path." God is always speaking. He is always leading, guiding, and directing, even when it seems we are alone. When we listen and welcome His presence, gladly, clearly, and plainly God speaks. There is no better mentor, motivator, or coach!

The scriptures tell us God and Adam shared a close and intimate relationship. This is evident in the fact that when God made other creatures, he consulted with Adam. It is recorded in Genesis 2:19-20 "the LORD God formed all the wild animals and all the birds of the sky from the ground. He brought them to the man (Adam) to see what he would call them, and the man chose a name for each one. He gave names to all the livestock, all the birds of the sky, and all the wild animals." It is apparent that God, the creator of the universe, loved Adam. He gave him authority, rule, and dominion over everything, allowing him to give names to His creations. God trusted Adam, and wisely, Adam cherished his time spent with God.

A relationship with God must be guarded and protected. Lucifer desires nothing more than to destroy that connection. Satan is the enemy and hater of men and women that never sleeps. He looks for every chance and opportunity to defeat God's warriors and champions. Tirelessly, he looks for a chink in the armor or the smallest breach in the wall. The writer admonishes us in 1Peter 5:8-9, "Stay alert! Watch out for your great enemy, the devil. He prowls around like a roaring lion, looking for someone to devour. Stand firm against him, and be strong in your faith." The devil will use and resort to any and every possible trick and tactic. He does not fight far. He will do anything to win. Patiently, he waits. He knows when we are disconnected and communication is limited, twisted, and distorted. He knows when we are vulnerable. He knows when we have not been intimate and close to the Holy and Eternal One by spending time with our God in prayer. When the communication between us and God is poor, we lack the sharpness of skills, understanding, and coordination of moves to dodge Satan's jabs and blows. As a result, we get pummeled by his attacks, leaving the ring scarred, battered, and unnecessarily bruised. When we do not spend time with God by studying His word, meditation, fasting, and prayer, we are woefully unprepared to face our enemies, and fight the fiercest of battles.

Like it or not, we are all in a fight. There is not a single day that passes that we have not had to fight. Our daily battle is not just any fight. Whether you know it or not, we are fighting for our lives, physically and spiritually. We have a tireless, merciless, and unwavering enemy, Satan. He is always working, plotting, planning, and scheming to destroy each of us. The scriptures tell us in Job 1:6-7, "One day the members of the heavenly court came to present themselves before the LORD, and the Accuser, Satan, came with them. Where have you come from?" The LORD asked Satan. Satan answered the LORD, "I have been patrolling the earth, watching everything that's going on." The Accuser (Satan) watches, waits, plots, plans, and then attacks. Make no mistake he is not a little man in a red suit with a pitchfork. He is a powerful spiritual being. About Lucifer the scriptures record in Ezekiel 28:14, "I ordained and anointed you as the mighty angelic guardian. You had access to the holy mountain of God and walked among the stones of fire." We cannot defeat him on our own. We need a good corner man. I recommend the Lord Jesus. There is none better. He will always provide perfect and divine counsel, because He knows the schemes of the enemy.

Since the garden, Satan has used deceptive and clever tactics to move us away from God. From the beginning, God gave clear instructions to man and woman. Unmistakably, God established a clear "Do Not Enter Zone". However, through tricky and cunning, Satan sabotaged the perfect union and relationship Adam and Eve enjoyed with God. Scripture tells us in Genesis 2:15-17, "The LORD God placed the man in the Garden of Eden to tend and watch over it. But the LORD God warned him, "You may freely eat the fruit of every tree in the garden— except the tree of the knowledge of good and evil. If you eat its fruit, you are sure to die." The man had complete dominion over the entire garden. There was nothing withheld from him except one specific tree. His obedience ensured peace, joy, contentment, and a perfect relationship with his creator. Man would live forever perfect union and harmony with God spiritually, and his body would never grow old or decay. Eternally, he would remain God's man, ruler, and champion.

Hating mankind because of the love and favor God gave them; Satan devised a subtle plan to destroy the relationship shared between God and His prized creation. It was and still is the plan of Satan to see us weak, vulnerable, afraid, and disconnected from the source of our strength, power, and life. Satan knows that only when we are disconnected from God does he and his minions have enough power to knock us down. Then and only then are we vulnerable. Without the power of God's spirit, we cannot withstand or defeat the schemes and power of Satan. Let us not fool ourselves there is no time when we do not need Christ Jesus in our corner. We need Him every minute and every hour. He alone can help us win even the toughest fights. Without God, we do not stand a chance. From the beginning until this present moment, Satan's desire has not changed. He wants nothing more than for everything God loves to die! The words of the Lord Jesus are recorded in John 10:10 "The thief's purpose is to steal and kill and destroy. My purpose is to give them a rich and satisfying life." Satan is the thief. To achieve his objectives, he will use any and everything available.

The scriptures tell us in Genesis 3:1-7, "The serpent was the shrewdest of all the wild animals the LORD God had made. One day he asked the woman, "Did God *really* say you must not eat the fruit from any of the trees in the garden?"Of course, we may eat fruit from the trees in the garden," the woman replied. "It's only the fruit from the tree in the middle of the garden that we are not allowed to eat. God said, 'You must not eat it or even touch it; if you do, you will die." "**You won't die!**" the serpent replied to the woman. "God knows that your eyes will be opened as soon as you eat it, and you will be like God, knowing both good and evil." The woman was convinced. She saw that the tree was beautiful and its fruit looked delicious, and she wanted the wisdom it would give her. So she took some of the fruit and ate it. Then she gave some to her husband, who was with her, and he ate it, too. At that moment, their eyes were opened, and they suddenly felt shame at their nakedness. So they sewed fig leaves together to cover themselves."

God did not tell Adam and Eve about Satan. He only gave them instructions to follow. He provided them the knowledge and instructions necessary for them to accomplish the work and tasks He had given them. He gave them the tools necessary to maintain dominion where they had been placed. All they needed to do was obey. Because Satan was an already defeated enemy, all required of them was obedience. God only made them privy to what they needed to know. From this fact, we learn several things. First, God does not always inform us of His plans. But He does supply us with everything we need for success and safety. Second, if we maintain close communication with God, we will always find great comfort, strength, and forgiveness. We see the Lord's compassion even after Adam and Eve's disobedience. Pitying Adam and Eve's shame and embarrassment, the scripture says in Genesis 3:21, "And the LORD God made clothing from animal skins for Adam and his wife." With Christ in our corner, we cannot lose. The path to victory is in the hand and mind of God. Our focus must be on Christ. He is the hope of our lives and the source of our strength. He will protect us from the sneakiness of Satan. None of his tactics will succeed. We can take comfort in the words found in Isaiah 54:17, "No weapon formed against you shall prosper, and every tongue which rises against you in judgment, you shall condemn. This *is* the heritage of the servants of the LORD, and their righteousness *is* from me," Says the LORD."

Beginning with Adam, we as followers of the only true and living God have been engaged in a never-ending fight. Through a continuous series of ups and downs, knockdowns, and delays getting up from the canvas, Christ is still with us. We are in good company, protected, and secure. The title of Him who is always with us is The King of Kings, The Lion of the Tribe of Judah, The Almighty. There is no battle; He is not the victor. Because He is with us, He will ensure our victory, leading us on perfect paths. In every situation, we need Christ in the corner, coaching, encouraging, and cheering us forward. We are no match for Lucifer. We need Jesus. It is through His power, leading, and direction that we can withstand the schemes of the enemy. We cannot do it alone.

If you would allow me to be honest, I must confess, I have had far more than my share of scrapes, bruises, knockdowns, and momentary knockouts. There have been moments so difficult and fights so hard that I have wanted to stay down. I know personally what it feels like to be willing and ready to surrender. I know the loneliness of Christ not being in my corner. How glad I am to have Him. He has taught me the benefit, importance, and necessity of His presence. He has not only shown me His indescribable love, but He has taught me how to fight, not with carnal weapons, but with the mighty weapons of faith and the spirit. Satan might knock us down, but the greater one will lift us again to our feet. The writer says in Psalm 27:5, "For in the day of trouble He will conceal me in His tabernacle. In the secret place of His tent He will hide me. He will lift me up on a rock." I know the Lord our God is a promise keeper. He is faithful and true. Through my own trials and errors, I have come to know that the Lord Jesus is faithful, even when I have been unfaithful. I can attest and confirm that the words of the Psalmist are true in Psalm 103: 8-14 "The LORD is compassionate and merciful, slow to get angry and filled with unfailing love. He will not constantly accuse us, nor remain angry forever. He does not punish us for all our sins; he does not deal harshly with us, as we deserve. For his unfailing love toward those who fear him is as great as the height of the heavens above the earth. He has removed our sins as far from us as the east is from the west. The LORD is like a father to his children, tender and compassionate to those who fear him. For he knows how weak we are; he remembers we are only dust."

No matter how many times we fall, there is still hope of victory. Getting knocked down does not mean we have to stay down. If you can look up, you can get up. Pain is part of the experience. Scrapes, scars, and bruises are indicators of a fight. We cannot avoid getting hit, beaten, and scarred. We may as well give it everything we have. Since we cannot avoid the fight, we might as well fight with everything we have. Through Christ, we have everything necessary to win. When you find yourself on the canvas, listen for the voice of the corner man. Jesus will instruct you. Listen to the words of Jesus in John 10:27-28, "My sheep listen to my voice; I know them, and they follow me. I give them eternal life, and they will never perish." He will give you the solution and the best course of action to secure every win. Jesus is always rooting for your victory. Before the battle begins, He declares you the winner. You need Him in your corner. There is no wiser choice or decision. If you have not done so already, will you make Him your choice today? I pray that the answer is "YES"!

LET US PRAY: Heavenly Father, we thank you for sending Jesus to be the coach and Savior of our lives. Through your Christ, we have limitless victory in the name of Jesus and a matchless connection to wise counsel in our corner. Help us, and teach us not to lean on our understanding. Teach us to fight by faith. Train us to focus and listen for your guidance as you lead us on the path to victory. We are what you called us to be, "Champions for Christ." Strengthen us, and teach us to exercise our faith. Bind our fear of every enemy that stands before us. Help us to know we are more than conquerors. Please, Lord, continue to be the source of our hope and the patient, and *wise counsel* in our corner, Amen.

CHAPTER EIGHT

Teach Me How to Counter

Beginning with the creation of man in the garden, God designed us for relationship and communication. When was the last time you spent time communicating with Him in prayer? In prayer, we allow God to draw close, whisper in our ear, and provide instruction for our next move. In a boxing match, at the end of a round, the bell rings. Each opponent retreats to his designated corner for rest, rejuvenation, repair, and a word of wise counsel. It is the coach who steps in and leads the care of the athlete's mind, body, and spirit. The writer in Proverbs 3:5-6 says, "Trust in the LORD with all your heart; do not depend on your understanding. Seek his will in all you do, and he will show you which path to take." Are you listening and relying on the matchless and indisputable counsel of Christ?

There is no greater or more important step than making Christ the center, focus, and hope of your life. If you have made the wisdom of Christ (His word) the counsel of your life, you have made a fantastic choice. If not, what logical reason can there be for not using the available power, gifts, and tools God has provided for you to succeed in every aspect of your life? Without God's leading and guidance, easily and quickly, we start moving and drifting in the wrong direction, far from the peaceful shore. We are ignorant of the plans and will of God. We cannot know the plans of God or how to please Him without communing with Him. The apostle Paul tells us in 1Corinthians 2:11-12, "No one can know a person's thoughts except that person's own spirit and no one can know God's thoughts except God's own Spirit. And we have received God's Spirit (not the world's spirit), so we can know the wonderful things God has freely given us."

We need the guidance and wisdom of a competent and well-seasoned coach capable of pushing, inspiring, and motivating us to get up and fight on, even when we want to quit and throw in the tool. Only through the counsel and power of God can we win and find victory in the hardest battles of life. With God, we are capable of achieving things never before imagined, and things we once believed impossible. We are assured by scripture in Isaiah 40:29-31, "He gives power to the weak and strength to the powerless. Even youths will become weak and tired, and young men will fall into exhaustion. But those who trust in the LORD will find new strength. They will soar high on wings like eagles. They will run and not grow weary. They will walk and not faint."

Until you go home to be with Christ, you are entangled in a constant fight against Satan, an expert in sly schemes. He is a master trickster. In the garden, he demonstrated one of his craftiest tricks. After thousands of years, he uses that same trick today. In the garden, he enticed Eve with knowledge, convincing her that she did not need God. Through his slyness, Lucifer made Eve believe she could be wise without God's presence. Successfully, Satan convinced Eve she could live and thrive without the input and counsel of God. Inarguably, Satan made Eve question the validity and accuracy of God's word. The evil one lured and enticed the creation to challenge the Creator's law and decree. He offered her an alternative, a question or challenge to God's declaration of "death," saying in Genesis 3:4-5, "You won't die!" the serpent replied to the woman. "God knows that your eyes will be opened as soon as you eat it, and you will be like God, knowing both good and evil." Listening to Lucifer's counsel, Eve rejected the sovereignty of God. Wrongfully, she wanted to remove God, govern herself, and become her own god. Satan convinced Eve to reject the assurance of life, and go against God's instruction, leading to the death of her and her husband, "Adam."

Through his trickery, Satan was able to achieve two objectives. First, he was able to bring sin into the world which brought separation from the holy presence of God. Second, through his deception, Satan initiated both the spiritual and physical death of our mortal bodies through sickness, disease, and decay. Because of the effects and damages of sin, Jesus says plainly, that men and women must be born again through the power of the Holy Spirit. Speaking about sin, the apostle Paul says in Romans 6:20-23, "When you were slaves to sin, you were free from the obligation to do right. And what was the result? You are now ashamed of the things you used to do, things that end in eternal doom. But now you are free from the power of sin and have become slaves of God. Now you do those things that lead to holiness and result in eternal life. For *the wages of sin is death*, but the free gift of God is eternal life through Christ Jesus our Lord." The Holy Spirit gives us God's power, equipping us for every fight and the ability to break the bonds, chains, and addictions of sin.

It is impossible to win a battle if you do not know or understand your enemy. Every fighter studies the opponent. God has given us the Bible as the manuscript, guide, and playbook. It is the source of power, instruction, and life. It is the irrefutable and incomprehensible word of God. Within its pages, we discover the moves, strategies, and counter to every attack of Satan. God's word teaches us how to win. Study and application develop and produce the warrior and champion mind. Through His word, we begin to see ourselves as God sees us, champions of Christ. From His word and through the power of Christ, we gain a new heart, mind, and regenerated spirit. We are told in Romans 8:1-4, "There is no condemnation for those who belong to Christ Jesus. And because you belong to him, the power of the life-giving Spirit has freed you from the power of sin that leads to death. The Law of Moses was unable to save us because of the weakness of our sinful nature. So God did what the law could not do. He sent his own Son in a body like the bodies we sinners have. And in that body, God declared an end to sin's control over us by giving his Son as a sacrifice for our sins. He did this so that the just requirement of the law would be fully satisfied for us, who no longer follow our sinful nature but instead follow the Spirit." Daily, we become more like Christ.

Through the power of God's spirit, we regain the knowledge of our true self and awaken our inward champion. When Christ's spirit lives in us, we are no longer slaves to sin or any of Satan's tactics, traps, or snares. On the contrary, we are more than conquerors. Romans 6:6-7 says, "We know that our old sinful selves were crucified with Christ so that sin might lose its power in our lives. We are no longer slaves to sin. For when we died with Christ, we were set free from the power of sin." Christ has set us free. Through His power, no weapon or plan of Satan can prosper in our lives. God has promised to protect us and be with us. He is leading, guiding, and directing our lives. There is nothing impossible in our lives if we believe we are what God has created us to be, His champions.

As the people and children of God, we can take courage from the words found in Deuteronomy 20:1-4, "When you go out to war against your enemies, and see horses and chariots and an army larger than your own, you shall not be afraid of them, for the LORD your God is with you, who brought you up out of the land of Egypt. And when you draw near to the battle, the priest shall come forward and speak to the people and shall say to them, 'Hear, O Israel, today you are drawing near for battle against your enemies: let not your heart faint. Do not fear or panic or be in dread of them, for the LORD your God is he who goes with you to fight for you against your enemies, to give you the victory." Go back to the diagram (The 5G Principle) in Chapter One. Take the first step onto the bridge of faith. Begin to renew your mind. It is now time to bridge the gaps in every area of your life. God is with you. He will guide you because He has ordained your destiny. So "Go" in faith and the power of Christ to victory. I want you to say to yourself, *"I am a Champion for Christ."*

Without Christ, men and women are beaten savagely throughout their lives. Foolishly, they punch, swing, and throw voracious but ineffective blows at a skillful and tactical enemy, Satan. Like many of us, they fight but lack the skills to win. The will to fight is not the same as mastery of technique, method, and style. No matter how good a fighter we envision ourselves to be, without conditioning and training; we quickly realize we lack stamina. After only a few rounds, we stagger and stall under the weight and demand of fatigue. Without testing it is easy to perceive ourselves as unbeatable. But in the heat of the battle, we discover we are ill-prepared to go the distance without spiritual conditioning developed through prayer, testing, and faith.

Back in the early 1990s, I sat with a famous visionary and rapper in a recording session at Echo Studio in California during the hardest fight of his life. Thinking of a military strategy, he wrote a song called "Bomb First". The premise of the song, get them before they get you. Sitting there, I visualized with your back against the wall, having lost everything, the ease of giving everything when your life is all you have left. In that moment I also realized that none of us really want to die. We all fight viciously to live. When challenged, we muster our greatest strengths and champion our beliefs. When given time to dream, we envision a place of peace shared with others. We want to live in a community. We desire to live connected, joined, and harmoniously. Satan works tirelessly to destroy, hinder, and deny us peace. In reflection, I am thankful for the lessons left by a twenty-five-year-old man, encouraging leaders to wage war with the pen and not with knives and guns. I pray that he rests in peace.

From a spiritual perspective, through trickery and deception, Satan "Bombed" first. He threw the first blow, pushing Adam and Eve into rebellion, disobedience, and sin. However, Christ is calling you back to the corner, so he can teach you how to "Bomb" back effectively. God never intended for Satan to get away with deceiving man and woman, initiating their spiritual and physical death. From the beginning, He had a plan to ensure our victory. For centuries, we have suffered the barrage and assaults of Satan. However, through God's power and grace, we are still standing, bloodied but unbowed. God has placed an indomitable spirit within us. He has made us champions. That deserves a "Hallelujah" moment. Now, say to yourself "God has made me from the good stuff." We can take confidence and pride in the fact that despite great difficulties, challenges, and significant losses, we are still in the fight. For that, we proudly and joyously worship our great and faithful God.

The rebellion and disobedience (sin) of Adam and Eve separated them from the presence of God. By right, He could have destroyed and abandoned them forever. But His love remained. Because of the unfailing love of God, there is good news. There is hope for every sinner. Even when we willfully sin like Eve and Adam, disobeying the clear warning of God, He will forgive us if we confess our faults and repent, turning back to righteousness. The scripture tells us in 1John 1:8, "If we confess our sins to him, he is faithful and just to forgive us our sins and to cleanse us from all wickedness." God sends the Holy Spirit to convict us, not condemn us. The Holy Spirit moves us to repentance. Satan uses the shame of our mistakes and sins to push us away from God. When we sin, Satan condemns us, making it hard for us to believe we are worthy of forgiveness. He torments and plagues us with guilt and shame. We are beaten down by the weight of sin, fallen like a fighter to the canvas.

I remember being in a corner room at Kaiser Permanente Hospital, standing over my father's bed, whose health was fading quickly. I heard him ask the Lord in a humbled voice, "What have I done to deserve this?" I could not interpret the conversation but rejoiced in the dialogue between him and Christ Jesus. I perceived the connection between his mind and the spirit. I witnessed the battle of the prizefighter and the intimate and personal conversation held in the corner. Witnessing the intricacies and tension of this exchange, I was reminded of the dialogue between Jesus and the Father as He hung between heaven and earth on Golgotha's hill at Calvary. It was on that hill, nailed to a rugged cross that Jesus bled, suffered, and died. Selflessly, He took on himself the weight and penalty of our sins. The scriptures tell us in Matthew 27:46, "About the ninth hour Jesus cried out with a loud voice, saying "Eli, Eli, Lama Sabachithani? That is, "My God, My God, why have you forsaken me?" This cry in agony was the result of feeling deserted, abandoned, and alone. Being the full and complete embodiment of holiness and perfection, God the Father cannot look on sin. In that moment, Jesus felt the sting and penalty of sin. He was alone. The face and presence of God (the Father) had turned away. However, because He loves us so much, Jesus took on himself the sins of the entire world so that whoever calls on Him can be saved. Jesus and no other paid the ultimate sacrifice for our freedom. If you have not chosen to accept Christ, now is the time. No matter who you have been dancing with through life, it is time to change partners. Let Jesus have the next dance.

If you have not allowed Christ to be in your corner, invite Him today. There could be no better choice. Christ knows you far better than you know yourself. He knows your skills, talents, gifting, and abilities. There is nothing about you He does not already know. There is no secret you can withhold or hide from him. The scriptures inform us that He knows our every thought before we form them. Remember, He said to the prophet in Jeremiah 1:5, "I knew you before I formed you in your mother's womb. Before you were born, I set you apart and appointed you as my prophet to the nations." Nobody knows you better than God. He created you and wants to coach, encourage, and lead you in every way. It is the desire, plan, and will of God that you succeed. Sometimes you get beat up. But, more times than not, you will emerge victoriously. You possess the DNA of greatness. The spirit of the living God is inside you. The scripture says in Genesis 2:7, "Then the Lord God formed man of dust from the ground and breathed into his nostrils the breath of life; and man became a living being." No other creature was made in the image of God. Also, no other creature's life came from the breath of God. You are special, unique, and priceless in the plan and mind of God.

No matter how difficult and exhausting the fight. God will patch you up and push you back into the fray. He is a good cut-man. He always has something in the corner to quench your thirst, revive, and mend the bruises of your soul. If we listen, Christ will tell us where and when to through our punches, landing the most powerful and effective blows. Following and obeying the word of God always leads to success. It never fails. God's word is the key. The Bible tells us of time when the disciples had been fishing with no success, even though they were skilled, professional, and master fishermen. However, Peter wisely obeyed the counsel of Christ. The scripture says in Luke 5:4-7, "When he had finished speaking, he said to Simon, "Now go out where it is deeper, and let down your nets to catch some fish." "Master," Simon replied, "We worked hard all last night and didn't catch a thing. But if you say so, I'll let the nets down again." And this time, their nets were so full of fish they began to tear! A shout for help brought their partners in the other boat, and soon both boats were filled with fish and on the verge of sinking."

I am here on one single mission. My single objective is to help you come to the knowledge that God has planned and purposed your life. He has ordained you to win and willed you to succeed. God has chosen you to be His champion. No matter what has knocked you down in the past, today is a new day. The darkness is fading away. The brightness and power of Christ are now shining.

LET US PRAY: Lord Jesus, we ask that you stir the Holy Spirit within us. Thank you for the words and messages on these pages. We are grateful for clearer understanding and light. Fill us with your goodness, grace, and mercy. Renew our hearts, minds, and spirits. As your children, help us to be your champions. We know you can change and turn any situation around for your glory. God, by your power, we have withstood the attacks and blows of the enemy. So often, we have been bloodied but unbowed. Lord, we ask that you give us more strength to endure the battle and teach us how to war and fight. Help us and show us how to counter-attack our enemy and win life's hardest challenges and battles, Amen.

CHAPTER NINE

Growing Up in the Fight

During my lifetime, I have had many experiences that helped develop within me a keen awareness and ability to relate to the struggles of others and the ability to cope with their sufferings and personal disasters. I have discovered that because of their struggles, hardships, and pain, many people have consistently wanted or expected me to fail or at least achieve and accomplish little. The Crabs in a barrel mentality is alive and well. I grew up in the inner city of South Central Los Angeles, considered the birthplace of West Coast gangs, Gangsta Rap, and the place where during the 1980s, drugs flown in from Columbia in the form of crack Cocaine ran rampant in the streets. Failure, prison, and death for many young Black men were a common reality. The deliberate flooding of Los Angeles streets with Cocaine created a climate of increased violence, family breakdown, high incarceration of Black males, countless premature deaths from violence, drug overdose, and the displacement of thousands of minority children, forced to enter group homes, foster care, and child protective services.

Where I grew up, bullets had no name on them. Frequently, stray bullets claimed the lives of countless victims deliberately and unintentionally. Sadly, death and loss became so common that random killings were normal, producing a feeling of expectancy and numbness. Loss and funerals became just a part of "Life in the Hood". On any day you could drive down the main avenue and see candles, balloons, empty liquor bottles, and pictures of people that passed away. The sound of ambulances, police sirens, EMTs, Fire trucks, and the chopping of wind from low flying helicopters, echoed nightly throughout our community. Many places have been so devastated and impacted by senseless and recurring violence that certain parks, corners, and spaces on sidewalks have become normal gathering points to meet, drink, smoke, BBQ, and reminisce about lost loved ones.

Some families had or created the financial position to move out and away from the ghetto, but for the much less fortunate living in economic disparity, the hood remained home. With limited options, the best many of us could do was attempt to survive, keep a calm and leveled head, and navigate while in the eye of the storm around us. Calmness never came easy when forced to keep your head on a constant swivel. Every day brought new uncertainty. It was hard to find a safe zone or place either physically or mentally when everywhere you looked was a reminder that someone had lost their life far too prematurely. Every day began with a prayer for protection and traveling grace as we dared to venture out to begin the daily grind, searching for a way out of poverty and into a brighter future.

If you are living in poverty or a situation that you desperately want to be removed from, no matter where you are, I want to encourage you. No matter your circumstance, I need you to know, God can and will lift you out of the pit of poverty, despair, and hopelessness. Nothing is too hard for God. Whatever you can imagine and believe, God can do it. The only thing that limits the move and power of God in our lives is faith. Trust God. Believe that He can, and He will. Even when you cannot feel Him or perceive His presence, know that He is there. He is working it out for you. Faith is the unwavering confidence, knowledge, and belief that God will do what might seem impossible. If He can separate the lakes, rivers, seas, oceans, and streams, He can create a miracle in your life as well. Walk by faith, and God will create the path for your escape. When God opens the door of opportunity, be courageous and take that necessary step of faith, and move forward.

The scripture tells us that our lives will be as we believe. If you can believe it, it can be yours. I want you to close your eyes and picture you and your family living in a space and place of safety, abundance, and peace. Stop for a moment. Hold that vision in your mind. What does that place look like? You must have a clear image and vision of what you want for yourself and your family. Remember, only you know what is right for you and your loved ones. No one else can give you a vision. Only you can tailor your thoughts to match your taste, desires, and needs. Can you see you and your loved ones there soon? If you can see it and believe it, God will help you make it a reality. He will provide you with the direction and guidance to get there if you trust Him. He will supply you with everything you need, including the necessary direction and guidance. However, you have to do the work and prepare. The journey of a million miles begins with the first step. Every day is an opportunity to move another step closer to the situation of your desires. I am not telling you what I heard but what I know. Like you, I have beaten the odds. I am a living testimony to the power and grace of God. My life's story is irrefutable evidence that nothing is impossible, and odds mean nothing when God is the author of the story.

Labeled "THE JUNGLES," filmed in the notorious movie "Training Day" starring Denzel Washington, my community remains stagnant, plagued, and without a solution to end the senseless acts of violence and death still perpetuated as a product of gang culture. I am confident the spirit of death has attached itself to this geographic area. Innumerable are the lives of young Black men snatched weekly. I am only one of the few recognizing a community in need of freedom from the power of Satan and his allurement of worldly pleasures, materialism, sexual impurity, and depravity of every kind. Nothing can help and change this repeated cycle of depravity and loss but total and complete freedom from the spiritual chains of the evil one. Only through the power of God's word is this possible. Only through His word comes saving faith, deliverance, and freedom from the power of sin, and the possibility of spiritual development and maturity. I would not wish my experiences on anyone else. However, God chose this path to bring me to adulthood and present me as a survivor. He orchestrated a unique way of allowing me to experience His grace and mercy. Amazingly, He has sustained and kept me all the way.

Because of all God has done in my life, I feel an overwhelming responsibility to give myself away. I am compelled to honor Him by preaching, teaching, and writing books like this for one unwavering purpose, to reach this current and future generation of people "REACHING FOR LIFE" through Christ. God has given me a new life. He kept me in and through the storms. He saved me. He redeemed me. He loved me when I did not know how to love myself. Through Christ, I have been allowed to lead by example through my actions and ministry of presence. Today, I serve Him in word and deed. Because Christ lives in me, I am compelled to carry myself as humbly yet as a fearless man of God within my community. I am a living witness, example, and testimony to what God can and will do with a life surrendered and yielded to Him.

Briefly, I would like to share some of my struggles and challenges growing up in a broken family and devastated community. In my neighborhood, certain gangsters with itchy trigger fingers would roam the streets searching for someone to shoot. At age fifteen, when the movie "Colors" was popular, I was the victim of police brutality simply because I lived in one of the gang neighborhoods depicted in the movie. During that era, countless beatings similar to Rodney King's went anonymous and untelevised or made primetime TV. My childhood was filled with stress, but God kept me through it all. Kids like me living in my community were considered outcasts, forgotten, unwanted, and destined to become drug dealers and criminals. Police harassment was a normal reality. There was no way to avoid or escape it.

During a routine traffic stop in 1989, police, those sworn to protect and serve, deviously placed drugs (a 5-0 Cocaine rock) on me in an attempt to charge me with a Felony. I was arrested and taken to the Los Angeles Southwest Station. I was being charged with possession and intent to distribute illegal drugs. However, God would not let it be so. By His grace, He intervened and blocked the work and plan of Satan. He had a greater plan and purpose for my life. There was an officer at the station who knew me from a child. He took the two crooked police officers that had arrested me into a room. Shortly, all three officers exited the room, and I was released from my holding cell. By His amazing grace; I am free, alive, and have a clean record. All I can say is, "If it had not been for the Lord" on my side, where would I be? This traumatic experience will be with me for the rest of my life. However, God turned a tragedy into testimony. I tell this story as evidence of God's power and ability to save and deliver.

For the record, let me be clear. I support the efforts of the good police officers that commit their lives to keep others safe from harm, criminal activity, and bodily violence. However, I am vehemently opposed to crooked, evil, and diabolical police officers' willingness to ruin the lives and future of innocent young men because of their socio-economic status, ethnicity, and demographic surroundings. Let it be welcome understood, I will fight to the death against any police or authority attempting to wrongfully deny or deprive me or others of the right and opportunity to experience the best and fullest possible life. I have never wanted to see the inside of a jail cell or prison. There is no badge of honor in that nor do I respect those who glory such ambitions. I have always valued my freedom, having high dreams and aspirations. I have always remained committed and determined to someday attain and enjoy my piece of the American pie, to include receiving my Ph.D.

Today I am a champion for Christ. By His grace and mercy, I live in victory. God has been so gracious and kind. He has opened so many doors, and allowed me to experiences so many wonderful things. He has prospered me beyond measure. It for that reason that I live my life in a way that serves as an example and testament to those around me, that with God all things are possible. Quite often I say that if I were a West Coast rapper, I would be the only Old-School rapper that still lives in the hood. Because of that reality, I still see the daily effects of drugs in people's lives and the devastation of hardened hearts. Consistently, I witness kids participating in activities that lead to their early demise, the result of being undisciplined and raising themselves. Sadly, without men willing to stand up and lead, many families, children, and communities will remain in ruin and on tragic course for destruction.

From the beginning, I was labeled an underdog, unlikely to succeed. But to the surprise of the naysayers, I have beaten the odds and won the fight. I am alive in Christ and freed from sin and the carnal captivity of the world. All thanks be to God. When God has a plan for your life and future, no evil weapon against you will prosper. When God is with you, nothing can stand against you. The only opinion or plan that matters is God's. We must all believe as God believes. What He says is truth. He alone knows our future. He has declared in His word that you are His, and He will keep you and redeem you if you obey and trust in Him. Allow your mind to be renewed with the mind of Christ. It is time for you to come out of captivity and into the newness of life and spirit. Hear the admonishment of the prophet in Isaiah 55:6-7 "Seek the LORD while you can find him. Call on him now while he is near. Let the wicked change their ways and banish the very thought of doing wrong. Let them turn to the LORD that he may have mercy on them. Yes, turn to our God, for he will forgive generously."

If you can see yourself living beyond your current conditions, then say this prayer:

"Lord Jesus, you can give me hope in my hopelessness and vision in my valleys. Whatever you allow me to see, you can make it come true. Whatever I believe, you will allow me to receive. Open new doors for me to walk through and close the chapters of my past. I am hopeful for a brighter future because you are with me. The best is yet to come. With joy in my heart and praise on my lips, I now walk in the newness of life. Let me walk in faith, assurance, and greater confidence in you. I pray this prayer in victory. By your power, I will walk out of my valley and into the purpose you have for my future. I thank you now and praise you in advance, in Jesus name, Amen."

CHAPTER TEN

It Is ShowTime

When Satan attempts and throws a jab, let God's word and the spirit of discernment block and shield you from his attack. When fighting such a skilled and calculating opponent, you need the Holy Spirit to teach you how to bob and weave, positioning you to defensively anticipate and avoid his every move. With God's leading, you will always know when, where, and how to "Bomb" back! Stay connected and covered by the Holy Spirit. When Christ is in your corner, no matter your mistakes in the past, you have the same resources as a newly trained fighter. Communicating with your corner equips you with needed and necessary wisdom, insight, and strategy. In the past, countless times you raised your hands in an act of defense, only to find yourself flat on the canvas, lifeless like a fish being weighed for sale. Listening to Christ always makes the difference. With new focus, loss will no longer be your story. The tides have turned, changed in your favor. With new vision and perspective, you have been reconnected to life, strength, and the eternal source of power. Now, because you are in Christ, dedicated, focused, and without distraction, you can and will defeat every opponent, and win life's greatest battles.

Christ has created you to be His champion, giving you dominion over every aspect of this world. Jog, sprint, or run the longer route God has planned for you. Take courage in knowing, God has already mapped the course you are on. Take the plunge bravely. Swim to the distant shore through the rough seas of sorrow. Emerge from the waters of challenge and experience tougher, stronger, more capable, and fit for the fight. Walk boldly through deceit, deception, and discouragement of fake and so-called friends, foes, and family. Keep your mind stayed and focused on God. He is the unfailing source of your strength. He made you a winner, not because you deserve it or have earned it. He created you to win because he loves you unconditionally. The scriptures tell us in Isaiah 54:10, "Though the mountains are shaken, and the hills are removed, yet my unfailing love for you will not be shaken, nor my covenant of peace be removed," says the Lord, who has compassion on you." We are further encouraged by the words in Roman 8:37-39 saying, "No, in all these things we are more than conquerors through him who loved us. For I am convinced that neither death nor life, neither angels nor demons, neither the present nor the future, nor any powers, neither height nor depth, nor anything else in all creation, will be able to separate us from the love of God that is in Christ Jesus our Lord."

Walk back into the ring; the fight is not over. You are a champion. Christ declared you the winner, victorious at your creation. Christ will mend your brokenness and heal the wounds of the past. Through the wisdom and counsel of Christ, you will reach higher heights and the top of the mountain. There is no journey God has placed you on that He is not aware of the challenges, difficulties, and struggles. He has prepared and equipped you for the task. All you have to do is believe. Soon you will realize your struggles have been developing you for a more significant moment. Now, through the power of Christ, become that Champion!

No power will come against you greater than the power that lives within you. The enemy may have power, but Christ Jesus has all power. For our benefit, the writer records in Matthew 28:18-20, "Jesus came and told his disciples, "I have been given all authority in heaven and on earth. Therefore, go and make disciples of all the nations, baptizing them in the name of the Father and the Son and the Holy Spirit. Teach these new disciples to obey all the commands I have given you. And be sure of this: I am with you always, even to the end of the age." Trust in the

Lord. He will help you, giving you immeasurable and countless victories. You will discover that every victory will give hope to others. You no longer fight alone. You have the power of Heaven with you. Your enemy's power is limited. However, the Holy Spirit, the source of your strength, is limitless.

Every punch you throw, now throw in faith. Keep your mind focused on the truth of the word of God, which declares that you are more than a conqueror. Not one blow of Satan will go unchecked or unanswered. Soon the acclaim of your faith and fighting spirit will become renowned. You will become recognized and known as a man/woman of tremendous and effective faith and power. In the presence of Christ within you, demons will tremble to recognizing opponents do not last long in combat because your God is with you, even when you do not believe. The writer says in Deuteronomy 1:30-31, "The LORD your God who goes before you will himself fight for you, just as he did for you in Egypt before your eyes, and in the wilderness, where you have seen how the LORD your God carried you, as a man carries his son, all the way that you went until you came to this place." You will be a living testament and story, showing how God takes messes and turn them into transforming messages.

The source of your strength is Christ and Him alone. Christ Jesus is the secret weapon. Your enemies and opponents did not see your training and boot-camp regiment. They could not see your preparation for the greatest and most difficult fights. Your secret weapon: Morning scriptures reading, Daily Devotionals, Bible Study, regular church attendance, fasting, prayer, and daily communication with Christ, the coach in the corner. They could not know that Christ teaches us how to get light, cut, and lean for the fight. It is time to exercise and strengthen our faith through devotion and daily consecration of time with God in prayer. The announcer is speaking. Spectators are seated. The bell is about to ring. It is Showtime! The fight for the life God intends and meant for you has begun.

Forget the past and forgive yourself. Let go of the bondage and baggage holding you. You cannot change the past. It is time to move on, forward and upward. There is nothing in your past that God holds against you. God was aware of everything before you did it. He is the God of all knowledge, past, present, and future. However, because of His love, God does not keep a record of His children's mistakes, misdeeds, or wrongs. We can take comfort in the words found in Psalm 130:3, "LORD, if you kept a record of our sins, who, O Lord, could ever survive? But you offer forgiveness that we might learn to fear you." God's love for His people is wondrous and unexplainable. He is a great, wondering, and loving father. The writer in Micah 17:18-20 asks the question, "Where is another God like you, who pardons the guilt of the remnant, overlooking the sins of his special people? You will not stay angry with your people forever because you delight in showing unfailing love. Once again, you will have compassion for us. You will trample our sins under your feet and throw them into the depths of the ocean! You will show us your faithfulness and unfailing love as you promised to our ancestors Abraham and Jacob long ago." God wants you to win at all costs. There is nothing good He will not give to you. All you have to do is be courageous and believe.

LET US PRAY: Lord, we thank you for bringing us all the way. You have never left us nor forsaken us. We have been blinded by this world through a lack of your Word in our lives. We thank you for finding us and showing us how important we are to you. Help us to see ourselves as you see us. Strengthen our faith as we step back into the ring. Make us your gladiators, warriors, and champions for your glory and the Kingdom of Heaven. We renounce the lies of the evil one. We embrace your purpose and plans for our destiny. We believe in your power to transform our lives, making them immensely better. We receive the love you have fixed on us. Guide us, keep us, and direct every punch we throw at the enemy. Make our battle cry eternally be, "No God, No Glory!" Lord, help us to shine like new stars and the brightest suns. Make us Champions for Christ. In the name of Jesus, we pray, Amen.

CHAPTER ELEVEN

Victory is Yours

It would be untrue to say that life is easy or not without unforeseen and sometimes crippling challenges. I would be wrong not to admit that life at times will box you in, cut you off, and pin you in a corner. In these moments, we then realize there is nowhere to go. There is no more room to retreat. Our only available choices are fight or die. These are the times we are forced to face whatever stands before us. The decision rest with us, fight or be defeated. Go down swinging or surrender and be completely devoured and destroyed. All along, this has been Satan's demonic will and plan. He wants us defeated. He wants us to fall for his tricks and diabolical schemes. Cleverly, he plays on our minds, specifically during tough and challenging times. He presents to us images that are not at all true. He clouds our thoughts. Like a lion's roar, we are distracted from the truth by Satan's tactics, moving our focus and attention from the word of God. The lie of the enemy becomes more believable than God's truth.

Satan understands the biggest wars we will ever fight or on the battlefields of our minds. Knowing the power of our thoughts, that is where he wages war against us. Being a fallen angel, Lucifer knows God's word better than we do. He knows intimately the truth found in Matthew 8:13; then Jesus said to the centurion, "Go your way; and *as you have believed,* so ***let it be done*** for you." On many occasions of our lives, one day everything is fabulous. The next day we feel overcome, consumed, and enveloped the demonically conjured mental fog of despair. Strategically, Satan removes God, His Word, and His power from our perspective, view, and sight. Like a mirror in a carnival's Funhouse, he distorts reality. He tricks us into believing his lies in contrast to God's unwavering and eternal truth. For a lack of a better word, let's call it the devil's "Fabulous Fog" that blinds us and clouds our minds so that we cannot seem to find and navigate our way. Through his tricks and masterful devices, he rocks and shakes our faith. He knows that when the "mind is not right, nothing is right." Because we are fighting against a spiritual being, this spiritual battle cannot be won with the frustration of physical flying fists. It must be fought in the spirit! The writer in Ephesians 6:10-17 reminds us:

> "Be strong in the Lord and in his mighty power. Put on all of God's armor so that you will be able to stand firm against all strategies of the devil. We are not fighting against flesh-and-blood enemies, but against evil rulers and authorities of the unseen world, against mighty powers in this dark world, and evil spirits in the heavenly places. Therefore, put on every piece of God's armor so you can resist the enemy in a time of evil. Then after the battle, you will still be standing firm. Stand your ground, putting on the belt of truth and the body armor of God's righteousness. For shoes, put on the peace that comes from the Good News so that you will be fully prepared. In addition to all of these, hold up the shield of faith to stop the fiery arrows of the devil. Put on salvation as your helmet, and take the sword of the Spirit, which is the *word of God.*"

Satan loves to use the pain and trauma of the past, abuse, neglect, childhood pain, and the absence of Godly instruction, direction, counsel, and guidance to lure the unsuspecting to a quick and unnecessary death. The devil's work is in complete contrast to God's will. God wants us to have purpose and victory in every aspect of life.

Praying for another believer, expressing the heart of God, the writer in 3 John said, "Beloved, I pray that you may prosper in all things and be in health, just as your soul prospers." Through the spirit of wisdom, the writer in Proverbs says. "Corrupt people walk a thorny, treacherous road; whoever values life will avoid it. Direct your children onto the right path, and when they are older, they will not leave it." God has always desired the very best for each of us. Every experience that has led you to question the love of God is the work of Satan. The Father's very nature and character is love. No matter what you have been through, focus on the fact that you are a survivor, and that God has been with you every step of the way. You are a living testimony. You are the evidence of His sustaining power. By His power and faithfulness, you are still alive, Hallelujah!

Growing up without a mother or father in the home, we learn to survive, even at times feeling and being starved for love. We learn to live and survive with broken and missing pieces. With broken hearts, tear-stained cheeks, and the deep pain of regret, forced to witness the perceived fairytale of other intact and perfect families, we carry on. Sadly, broken homes contribute to the creation of wounded and broken souls and spirits. The world is filled with the walking wounded, struggling, and challenged to live just another day. However, that may not be your story. In contrast, you might have had a picture-perfect home life like the fictional character Bruce Wayne "Batman," losing your parents tragically, consequently denied the love, care, and necessary guidance and leadership required for spiritual development. Nevertheless, no matter the category or camp you fall into, the lack of a foundation in Chris makes life's challenges, demands, and crises far more overwhelming without the benefit of proper direction and instruction.

As a survivor, you find ways to cope and carry on. With time you learn to adapt and manage the situation you find yourself in. Sadly, we mask the pain, filling our lives with every imaginable possession of the world, but remain empty. We can have spouses, children, pets, and friends but still feel we have no one to talk to and alone. So many times in life, we feel down, lost, and broken. Pain and heartache come in so many forms. All too familiar is the loss of sibling, spouse, child, parent or friend. The loss of a loved one coupled with the breakdown or failure of a close or important relationship can push us to the brink. Desperation moves us closer and closer to the point of no return. Many times, when things seem unredeemable, these are the moments when we want to throw in the towel. When all seems lost and the hope of light shining impossible, we can bear no more punishment. We just want it to stop. Desperately, we want a relief. If you have ever felt the bite and sting of loss, tiredness, and defeat, you should be able to agree that at least once or twice you have contemplated giving up and just quitting. There is no shame or judgment in that; we all have!

The adage says, "Quitters never win, and winners never quit!" I know you are saying, "Yes, Pastor Neal, I have heard that before. But you have no idea what I have been through, nor do you know what I am going through now!" I got it. I hear you loud and clear. I realize that life can beat us down. I am mindful of the fact that life can hit us with blows leveling us, causing us to want to stay down on the canvas and never get up. However, although that is true, it is no excuse to quit. God has made us tougher and stronger than the devil wants us to realize. The Lord our God is with us. He will never let us be destroyed by the wilds of the enemy. To defeat us, Satan needs us to be willing participants. He needs us to believe his lies, abandoning the truth of God's perfect and precious word. The devil is a liar! We must stand strong in the power of our God's might. We cannot turn to drugs, alcohol, illicit sex, and carnal devices to dull the pain. That is not God's will. Come out of that sunken and dark place. Satan has already been defeated! You cannot lose hope. You cannot rest and sleep there in that place of depression, loneliness, isolation. Turn to Jesus. He will strengthen you, lifting you into his light. There is no depth too low or place too dark that Christ Jesus cannot reach. In the name of Jesus, I decree that you come out of that dark place, this very moment!

I have to ask a very serious and important question. This question is for a special group. Have you ever felt like enough is enough? Have you ever said, "I'm tired, and I want out!" Have you ever thought to yourself, this life is too difficult, challenging, and unfulfilling? Have you said to yourself, "There is nothing good in this world; why should I keep trying?" Are you a habitual pill popper to dull the pain? Are you like me, one of those has taken a gun and contemplated a quick exit? Are you one of those who cannot figure out, find a good enough reason, or a way to move past the darkness? Are you contemplating ending it all by suicide? If so, you are not alone. You are one of millions. Daily, countless men and women think about it. Scores make attempts. According to statistics, 1.2 million people attempted suicide this year. Sadly, countless others make plans and follow through with those plans. In the year 2020 alone, nearly 46,000 people committed suicide in the United States. This is not the plan or will of God. However, this is exactly the plan and will of Satan. His desire from the beginning has been to kill and destroy God's most valued and prized of all creation, man and woman. He cannot kill or destroy us on his own. If that were possible, he would have destroyed all of humanity long ago. However, through trickery, lies, and deception, just like he tricked Eve in the garden, he lures us away from God's truth. He paints a deceptive picture or presents an illusion of hopelessness, hoping we surrender, quit, stop resisting and fighting, and chose a quick and tragic end. Remember, the devil came to steal, kill, and destroy. Christ Jesus came to give peace, joy, and eternal life.

If you are struggling, I pray in the name of Jesus that you would resist the urge and desire to end your life. God loves you. Jesus paid the matchless price on Calvary so that you might live and have the abundance of life. He wants nothing more than to bless, heal, and prosper you in every way. Every thought, idea, and suggestion not of God comes directly from your enemy Satan! He is not your friend. He can never be trusted. Every word that he speaks is a lie. He cannot tell the truth. Every word that comes from him is a lie, and incompatible with the word of God. There is no such thing as a little "white" lie. Either it is the truth or a LIE! Poison is still deadly no matter how sweet. Satan will use any and every trick to lure us into us own destruction. He is the father of lies and deception. Please do not fall for his tricks, deceitfulness, and lies. I want you to know that you are not in this fight alone. God is with you. You have a purpose, and the power of God lives in you if you have received the Holy Spirit. If you have not, ask Him to come into your heart. Satan comes only to kill. God has come to give you abundant and eternal life. Satan hates you because God loves you. You were created to create life. Satan desires that you abort your gifts, and end your life. He is a murderer. He is the author and instigator of every unrighteous war and unnecessary death around the world.

Pain is a part of life, but God has given us His spirit to endure challenges and trials. Every trial has a purpose. Satan works strategically to distort this truth. Through demonic tactics, the devil attempts to convince you to despise the life God has given you. He distorts reality. He twists perceptions. He exaggerates every scenario. He blinds us to the presence and sovereignty of God. Satan desires that you put an end to your precious life rather than end the work and power of sin in your life. Lucifer would rather you die in sin than live in victory. We know he is a liar because the scriptures remind us in Romans 6:6-11, "We know that our old sinful selves were crucified with Christ so that sin might lose its power in our lives. We are no longer slaves to sin. For when we died with Christ we were set free from the power of sin. And since we died with Christ, we know we will also live with him. We are sure of this because Christ was raised from the dead, and he will never die again. Death no longer has any power over him. When he died, he died once to break the power of sin. But now that he lives, he lives for the glory of God. So you also should consider yourselves to be dead to the power of sin and alive to God through Christ Jesus." As stated before, the purpose of this book is to take you deeper in your faith and knowledge of the Lord Jesus, and to challenge you to open your physical and spiritual eyes.

Like a fighter in the ring, through these pages, with spiritual smelling salts, Christ has lifting you from the canvas. He wants you on your feet and back in the fight!

Now, to those under the legal age, adolescents forced into facilities and homes commissioned for your care but treated like cattle and cash cows, I feel your pain. Separated and often not knowing your biological parents can be overwhelmingly difficult, challenging, and hard. Being a client and nothing more than a symbol of money, it is reasonable to feel unloved. To all of you that from your earliest memories can only remember fighting, I know you are tired. But please, just hold on. You have to live! By the power of the living God, I declare in the name of Jesus that you will live and not die! I know at times you feel like a prisoner in a tight and crowded cell in your soul. Rightly, you feel enraged, being denied the help you need to deal with your pain and hurt. Nobody was there to stop you from being assaulted, molested, and raped. Nobody was there to protect you from those that claimed to love you but were the source of your most nagging nightmares. It is unfair that your closest friend or loved one died the way they did, leaving you alone to cope with the pain. But still, hold on!

How cruel it is when others disregard your pain, tell you "it's not that bad," or just get over it. It seems like Satan is winning, pounding you with pain and crushing blow after blow. It seems like nobody cares. The Devil is a Liar! I can assure you that God cares. He knows about your hurt. He is mindful of your pain. If you can only find the strength to cry out to Jesus, He will answer you. Let Him be in your corner. He will help you. The writer tells us in 1Peter 5:7, "Give all your worries and cares to God, for he cares about you." We also have the words of the Psalmist is Psalm 27:1-3, 10 "The LORD is my light and my salvation—so why should I be afraid? The LORD is my fortress, protecting me from danger, so why should I tremble? When evil people come to devour me, when my enemies and foes attack me, they will stumble and fall. Though a mighty army surrounds me, my heart will not be afraid. Even if I am attacked, I will remain confident… Even if my father and mother abandon me, the LORD will hold me close."

In this fight of life, there are always two coaches, opposing voices, Christ and Satan. One speaks to you about life, and the other encourages you to death and destruction, no matter how slyly. Nothing the devil says is true. He is a liar. When he says, take one puff, one hit, one shot, have one long, heated, and sensual night of passion with someone else, it will be alright. He has lied. He has tricked you. He will never tell you the penalty and consequence. He does not tell you of the trap of addiction. He does not tell of the pain of disease or the emotional and psychological damage of being unfaithful or physically attached to the wrong person. He does not tell you the penalty and price of sin. He neglects to reveal that the consequence of sin is death. There is always a hidden price to pay. Christ has and will never lie to you. He will never give or tell you a half-truth. He has said boldly, "Come to me, and I will give you rest for your soul." He has told you honestly, "I am the way, the truth, and the life." The writer says in Matthew 8:12, Jesus spoke to the people once more and said, "I am the light of the world. If you follow me, you won't have to walk in darkness because you will have the light that leads to life."

Satan is the prince of this world and hates the fact that mankind was created for God's glory. Lucifer despises the notion that Jesus loves you so much that he died to save us, and will never abandon you. No matter the situation or circumstance, Christ will stand by you and coach you through every attack and assault of the devil. The Lord God is always there. The devil is a master illusionist. His schemes and trick can be surprisingly convincing. However, they are merely parlor tricks. They are nothing more than fancy and well crafted delusions and lies. Satan cannot harm you. He can only do what the Lord permits and allows. No matter your situation, God will deliver you. Hold on and trust him. He is faithful and unfailing. It does not matter how we start in this life. More important is how when finish. No matter how small and humble the beginning, God can make us great. We can never forget David, who went from being a little anonymous shepherd boy to being hailed as the great giant killer, and celebrated king of Israel.

I would like to speak to all of the Lord's champions. God has given you His power and a blueprint to becoming victorious over your adversary. It is time to cast away every sin and transgression. It is now time to draw a line in the sand. Either chose Christ or not. The scripture tells us in Hebrews 12:1, "Since we are surrounded by such a huge crowd of witnesses to the life of faith, let us strip off every weight that slows us down, especially the sin that so easily trips us up. And let us run with endurance the race God has set before us." Let us stop listening to the lies of Satan and start believing wholeheartedly in what the word of God says about us. Even if you feel in bondage right now, you can be free. By the power of the Lord our God, and in the name of Christ Jesus, I command you to be free! By the power of the Living God, I break the bonds and hold of Satan. I command every demonic force and spirit that attempts to raise its head against the work and will of God to be cast down, back into the pit from whence it came, in the name of Jesus.

It is the will of God through Christ Jesus that you live victorious and free. God desires and wills that you have the abundance and fullness of life. We are reminded by the scriptures which read in Luke 4:17-21,

"The scroll of Isaiah the prophet was handed to him. He unrolled the scroll and found the place where this was written: "The Spirit of the LORD is upon me, for he has anointed me to bring Good News to the poor. He has sent me to proclaim that *captives will be released*, that the blind will see, that the *oppressed will be set free*, and that the time of the LORD's favor has come." He rolled up the scroll, handed it back to the attendant, and sat down. All eyes in the synagogue looked at him intently. Then he began to speak to them. "The Scripture you've just heard has been fulfilled this very day!"

Can you see yourself free? God has released you from the pain, hurt, and torment of your past if you will receive it. He has removed the scales from your eyes. Will you open your eyes? Let the new light shine where there was once darkness. If you have not accepted Christ as your personal Savior, I welcome you now to receive Him. We all need a Savior. Jesus, the Lord's Christ, is the only one that can fully and completely save. I encourage you to make the greatest decision and choice of your life. Accept the only hope and answer for all of humanity, Jesus, the Father's only begotten Son. Hear now the words in Romans 9:9-12,

"If you declare with your mouth, "Jesus is Lord," and believe in your heart that God raised him from the dead, you will be saved. For it is with your heart that you believe and are justified, and it is with your mouth that you profess your faith and are saved. As Scripture says, "Anyone who believes in him will never be put to shame." For there is no difference between Jew and Gentile—the same Lord is Lord of all and richly blesses all who call on him, for, "Everyone who calls on the name of the Lord will be saved."

Satan wants to keep your eyes blurry and clouded, unable to focus and see his tricks, tactics, and antics. Christ wants you to be clear-headed, focused, a victor, and a champion. Jesus has paid it all so that you can have it all. Come to Him now, and live in the newness of life. As he was speaking to His disciples, we can hear the words of the master recorded in Luke 16:4, Jesus says, "I have told you these things, so that in me you may have peace. In this world, you will have trouble. But take heart! I have overcome the world."

CHAPTER TWELVE

Claiming the Championship

Picture Christ as your Corner-man, whispering, "See yourself as a winner, a champion! Look past the pain, the hurt, and the crisis of life. Focus, concentrate, and remember you are facing an opponent I have already beaten. I am Christ, the Captain of the Heavenly Host. I am Christ, the Prince of the Armies of the Lord. I am Christ, the King of Kings and Lord of Lords. I am Jesus, the Eternal and undefeated one. I am your comforter, companion, and friend. I am your support, encourager, and coach. Now, get up. It is time to fight and win!"

Listen, you have what it takes to win. Satan will not fight fair. He will use every conceivable nasty trick. He will throw dust in your eyes. He will hit you before and after the bell. He will lie to you and taunt you with your past. He will definitely hit below the belt. However, do not lose heart. Do not bend or bow to this trickster. The power of God is in your corner. Because I am here, you have more than enough to achieve the task. Be encouraged by the fact that "The Spirit who lives in you is greater than the spirit who lives in the world."

In ever battle, even before it begins, you have to decide if you are going to win or not. The choice is yours. The power of life and death, success or defeat, is in your words and thoughts. Repeatedly the scriptures remind us that it is as we believe. Whatever we believe and say will be, so it will be. You can win. You were created to win. Not only has Christ Jesus gone before you to make the path straight, but He has also won the victory. All you have to do is believe. No matter where you are. No matter what you are going through, God has not forgotten you. He is there. He is with you. Christ has never lost a battle. He has poured His spirit on you. You have the spirit of a champion. He has equipped you with immeasurable (*dunamis*) capacity of power. The same power that raised Jesus from the dead lives in you. There is no reason for your defeat, unless you surrender and give up before the fight is over.

Satan knows that if he can capture your thoughts and keep you distracted, unfocused, and disconnected from the truth of God (His Word), he can manipulate, manage and limit the degree of power in your life. It is only through your free will and choice to accept and allow Christ's reign and authority in your life that you have access to His power. The power of God is only accessible and available to those that belong to Christ, children of the Living God. This power belongs only to those that walk in the light and are no longer in darkness. This power is reserved for those identified as children of the LORD of Lords, the Lord Jesus Christ. It is recorded in John 1:13; "He came into the very world he created, but the world didn't recognize him. He came to his own people, and even they rejected him. But to all who believed him and accepted him, he gave the right *to become children of God.* They are reborn—not with a physical birth resulting from human passion or plan, but a birth that comes from God."

It does not matter what you have done in the past. It does not matter where you come from. It does not matter if you do not know a lot about Him. He will accept and receive you, just as you are. Do you want His power? Do you want His Spirit to live inside you? Do you want to be equipped with everything you need to break the power of Satan and the chains of sin and bondage from your life? No matter what the Devil has told you. Every word is a lie! Remember, he is the father of lies. Every word he speaks is a lie. He cannot tell the truth, no matter how convincing it sounds. The truth is that God loves you and wants you to be His own. If you want God's spirit, power, and presence in your life, all you have to do is ask. Speaking to a group, Jesus said these words recorded in Luke 11:11-13; "You fathers—if your children ask for a fish, do you give them a snake instead? Or, if they ask for an egg, do you give them a scorpion? Of course not! So if you sinful people know how to give good gifts to your children, how much more will your heavenly Father give the Holy Spirit to those who ask him?"

Like a drunken fighter, you feel as if the weight and strain of carnality have you wobbly against the ropes. However, I challenge you to hold on, fight! You cannot give up. You cannot surrender. The fight is not over. I know the struggle can be exhausting. I know the required and necessary energy can be more than we are willing to give, but fight. Stay in the tussle. You are not the first, nor will you be the last required to give it all for a changed future. God wants you to win, but it demands sacrifice. Your destiny demands that you step back into the ring and lay it all on the line. Victory requires you to leave it all in the ring. It demands that you come back to the corner fully and completely spent. It demands that you tell God, "Here I am. Take all of me!" No matter the price, you want and need a breakthrough. You need God's power. You need a blessing that will transform and change your life forever.

In the Old Testament of scripture, we find a tremendous example of Jacob in trouble, desperation, and in need of a blessing. He needed a transformation, a breakthrough. We find Jacob determined and unwilling to remain the same, and in his circumstance. Resolved and determined, Jacob laid it all on the line, no matter the cost. The scriptures read in Genesis 32: 24-28; "a man came and wrestled with him until the dawn began to break. When the man saw that he would not win the match, he touched Jacob's hip and wrenched it out of its socket. Then the man said, "Let me go, for the dawn is breaking!"

But Jacob said, "I will not let you go unless you bless me." "What is your name?" the man asked. He replied, "Jacob." "Your name will no longer be Jacob," the man told him. "From now on, you will be called Israel because *you have fought with God and with men and have won.*"

Your struggles and challenges are all too familiar. Scripture is riddled with the stories of men and women and their difficulty in getting it right. However, it is also filled with the repeated themes of God's inconceivable grace, compassion, and love for His children. We are reminded in Psalms 103:8-12; "The LORD is compassionate and gracious, slow to anger, abounding in love. He will not always accuse, nor will he harbor his anger forever; he does not treat us as our sins deserve or repay us according to our iniquities. For as high as the heavens are above the earth, so great is his love for those who fear him; as far as the east is from the west, so far has he removed our transgressions from us." Like you, I once thought I was far beyond God's redemption. But, Praise God, Salvation cannot be earned. It is a gift from God to all that will receive it. We cannot do enough good to manipulate God's love for us or enough bad for Him to stop loving us. He loves us because He is love. To all that follow Christ Jesus and place their hope in Him, the apostle Paul assures us in Ephesians 2:8-10; "God saved you by his grace when you believed. And you can't take credit for this; it is a gift from God. Salvation is not a reward for our good deeds, so none of us can boast about it. We are God's masterpiece. He has created us anew in Christ Jesus, so we can do the good things he planned for us long ago." As we read further, Ephesians 2:1-10 gives us three reasons why God wants to save us. The first is to show His love (*hesed*). The second is to show His grace. The third is to show His workmanship through our doing good works.

Did you know that sin leads to physical and (spiritual) death? Sin separates us from the presence and power of God. Not some sin, but all sin separates us from God. Sin breaks God's connection, flow, and move, in, on, and throw us. To use a phone analogy, sin produces static in the line. If Satan is successful at distorting the image, vision, sound, and will of God, he can cause us to live and remain in deliberate and or unintentional sin, rebellion against our Father. Unbeknownst to many, repeatedly, we are predisposed to commit sins of omission (things we should do but do not) and commission (things we do but should not). Tactically, Satan works to convince us that small things are insignificant, unimportant, and inconsequential. He deceives many into believing that God winks or ignores small sins. That is a lie. God hates sin. Because He is completely holy, and completely righteous, He abhors all sin. All sin big or small distances His presence and spirit. That is the plan and will of Lucifer, the evil and deceptive one. The father of all lies and all that is unrighteous.

Satan's objective is to separate us from the source of life. Ultimately, that is his goal. He wants to kill you physically and spiritually. Knowing his time is limited, he wants you to someday join him in Hell. Do not fall for his trick, the lie that there is little and big sin(s). To God, all sin is the same. God hates sin and cannot be in the presence of sin. Because of His loathing for sin, He (God) wrapped Himself in flesh, manifested Himself in the person (flesh) of Jesus (God the Son), and suffered and died on Calvary to pay the penalty and price of sin. It stays to reason, if sin were such a small thing, God would not have left Heaven, become a man, and suffered the horrendous death of the Crucifixion. It was the loathing of sin, the love of humanity, and the unwillingness to allow His prized creation t o suffer the penalty demanded for sin that led the Son of God (God in the Flesh) to suffer the penalty of capital punishment reserved for criminals, death by exhaustion and asphyxiation of a cross on the hill of Golgotha. It is recorded in Romans 3:22, 25-26, "We are made right with God by placing our faith in Jesus Christ. And this is true for everyone who believes no matter who we are…God presented Jesus as the sacrifice for sin. People are made right with God when they believe that Jesus sacrificed his life, shedding his blood. This sacrifice shows that God was being fair when he held back and did not punish those who sinned in times past; for he was looking ahead and including them in what he would do in this present time. God did this to demonstrate his righteousness, for He is fair and just, and he makes sinners right in his sight when they believe in Jesus."

If you are living an unsaved, unrepentant, and unredeemed life, God regards you as one of the "Sons of disobedience." You are not a child of the light because you willfully choose to walk in darkness. You cannot say you are a child of God and live contrary to the will and ways of God. The scriptures assure us that we can know a tree by the fruit it bears. I cannot call an apple tree an orange tree if I do not see any sign of oranges. I must call it what it is, if I see physical evidence of apples growing. The same is true of a person's life. You cannot say you are a follower of Christ without any evidence. Now, let me be clear, I am not here to judge. For Thirty-eight plus years, I, too, was a "Son of disobedience." I did whatever I wanted to do. I walked fully in my debased and depraved nature. I did not have the spirit of Christ. The Bible teaches that all men and women are affected and cursed with a sinful nature because of Adam's disobedience, just like the first man and woman who had fallen in the garden. Acting like disobedient children, walking in our fallen nature, we all become "children of wrath," living as enemies toward God, deserving of the full magnitude of His judgment and punishment. However, because He loves us, He makes a way for our escape. He does not treat us as we should be treated. He extends His love and grace. The writer in Romans 5:6-11 says,

> "When we were utterly helpless, Christ came at just the right time and died for us sinners. Now, most people would not be willing to die for an upright person, though someone might perhaps be willing to die for an especially good person. But God showed his great love for us by sending Christ to die for us while we were still sinners. And since we have been made right in God's sight by the blood of Christ, he will certainly save us from God's condemnation. For since our friendship with God was restored by the death of his Son while we were still his enemies, we will certainly be saved through the life of his Son. So now we can

rejoice in our wonderful new relationship with God because our Lord Jesus Christ has made us friends of God."

I am a living witness to God's amazing and transformative power. Had you known me before Christ saved me, you would have witnessed the many problems, hurts, and pains of my decaying life. It was a dark and challenging period of internal struggles with temptation, lust, and a myriad of other sins. I had no real direction, nor could I find a sense of purpose. One day Jesus stepped in and freed me from all my pain. He saved me and transformed me from the crown of my head to the soles of my feet. Through the power of God, I learned how to fight. Through His spirit, I came to understand the reason, purpose, and significance of my battles and many struggles. However, God not only taught me how to fight but how to win. By His great and divine grace, Christ revealed to me that I was worthy of His love and that He came to save a wretch just like me. He came to set all captives free! By His amazing love, He revealed to me the power and magnificence of the apostle's words in 2Peter 3:3-10;

"I want to remind you that in the last day's scoffers will come, mocking the truth and following their own desires. They will say, "What happened to the promise that Jesus is coming again? From before the times of our ancestors, everything has remained the same since the world was first created." They deliberately forget that God made the heavens long ago by the word of his command, and he brought the earth out from the water and surrounded it with water. Then he used the water to destroy the ancient world with a mighty flood. And by the same word, the present heavens and earth have been stored up for fire. They are being kept for the Day of Judgment when ungodly people will be destroyed. But you must not forget this one thing, dear friends: A day is like a thousand years to the Lord, and a thousand years is like a day. The Lord isn't really being slow about his promise, as some people think. No, he is being patient for your sake. *He does not want anyone to be destroyed but wants everyone to repent.* But the day of the Lord will come as unexpectedly as a thief. Then the heavens will pass away with a terrible noise, and the very elements themselves will disappear in fire, and the earth and everything on it will be found to deserve judgment."

LET US PRAY: Thank you O sovereign and gracious king. How grateful we are for the favorable and acceptable year of the Lord. Through your loving-kindness and compassion, you have afforded us the time and space to receive and accept the only acceptable sacrifice for our redemption, our Lord and Savior Jesus. We are grateful that you are calling and gathering your sheep from near and far into your flock, leading them toward Heaven. Thank you for protecting and defending us from the attacks of our enemies. O God, teach us how to fight the good fight in your name. Eternal king, it is our prayer that we grow in grace and become your ambassadors, emissaries, and champions. We thank you in advance. It is you that has called us to be. It is in your name we pray, Amen!

Final Thoughts

I praise the Lord Jesus for helping me realize that being in the right relationship with Him is more important than all the wealth and wonders of this world. Coming out of my test, I have this testimony. I know with certainty that you can win life's battles equipped with God's limitless power. It is my most sincere and earnest desire that this book helps you realize and discover, as I have, that *Jesus came to save you* because "you are worth fighting for."

On this journey, in the toughest fights, guts, gloves, and superior athleticism will not be enough to secure the win. Natural talents, abilities, or animalistic determination will not suffice. In this fight, victory can only be secured through the power of the Holy Spirit. Your opponent is a crafty and superior strategist; only obedience to the instructions of your friend, companion, and Corner-man will give you the edge and advantage. Jesus has come that you might be free. He has come to ensure your success. He has come so that you can have life and the fullness and richness of peace. He has come so you might know and experience the fullness of joy.

As you fight for your place and battle to secure your belt, know I will be somewhere in the audience cheering. With popcorn in one hand and the other lifted in prayer, I will be asking God to cover you with His power, and to anoint you for the victory. I have won many personal victories, and have also accumulated my share of scars. But God has graciously allowed me to secure many champion belts along the way. Trusting and leaning on God has been the enduring secret to my success. He has blessed me beyond measure. Hope in Him, and I am confident that He will do the same things for you. Rely on Christ. He has already won the victory. Stand strong in the power of His might. Step into the ring. It is Showtime. The bell is ringing. Let's go, champ!

> **LET US PRAY:** Thank you, Lord Jesus, for this great and interesting journey through the pages of this book. I pray that the words and thoughts expressed on these pages have drawn the reader closer to you. I pray that this has been an exercise of instruction in how we should walk more by faith and not by sight. Help us all to become confident and determined to be champions for Christ. Teach us how to boldly step into the ring, knowing you are in our corner. Guide us to glory and fill us with the Holy Spirit's power. Guide us forever as we fight the greatest battles of and fights for our lives. O God, teach us and train us to fight, until that day we study war no more. Make us daily more and more like you. In Jesus' name, we pray. Amen!

www.ingramcontent.com/pod-product-compliance
Lightning Source LLC
Chambersburg PA
CBHW060035050426
42448CB00012B/3022